Free to Be Holy beautifully sets forth the grand Wesleyan vision of holiness. O'Reilly has provided an exemplary service to the wider church in opening afresh a door of our movement, which was once well-traveled but has become more difficult to find in the contemporary world. I heartily recommend this fresh treatment of this central theme, reminding all Christians that the church is called by God to reflect his character in the world.

—Timothy C. Tennent
Distinguished Professor of World Christianity
Asbury Theological Seminary

This book deserves to be read far and wide, and with great care. God wants us to be holy. He says so in Scripture. He doesn't want us to be legalists, perfectionists, judgmental, or spiritually self-absorbed. He wants us to be godly. As O'Reilly makes clear, this means that he wants us to be full of divine love for both God and our neighbors (indeed, even our enemies). It's time for us to stop making excuses for our apathy or opposition to this. Our witness to the gospel is at stake.

—Douglas A. Sweeney
Dean, Beeson Divinity School

Matt O'Reilly's book helps reorient misguided conversations to remind readers that holiness is about sharing in and embodying the divine character of the triune God in our daily lives. O'Reilly's pastoral heart is evident as he unpacks key scriptural passages with concern, care, and compassion. This book is bound to encourage readers—both inside and outside the church—to gain greater clarity that holiness is about being in loving relationship with God and the rest of humanity.

—Tammie Grimm
Associate Professor of Congregational Formation
Wesley Seminary (Marion, Indiana)

Free to Be Holy invites readers to reconsider the beauty of holiness on the Bible's terms. O'Reilly offers an accessible and engaging survey of the witness of Scripture and the invitation to a holy life, even to perfect love. He shows us that holiness is not a depressing burden we must take on, but a joyous invitation where we find true freedom to live as we were meant to live.

—Kevin M. Watson
Author of *Perfect Love: Recovering Entire Sanctification—The Lost Power of the Methodist Movement*

Far from being a study in legalism, or an encouragement for eager beaver Christians to become holier than thou, this is a solid treatment as to what real holiness, which God expects of his people, is all about. Highly recommended.

—Dr. Ben Witherington III
Amos Professor of New Testament for Doctoral Studies
Asbury Theological Seminary

Matt O'Reilly has given the church a profound gift with *Free to Be Holy*. Writing with the care of a pastor and the depth of a theologian, O'Reilly helps readers experience how holiness is not punishment but privilege; not a "have to" but a "get to." I look forward to using this resource with the people of Good Shepherd Church and I'm sure you'll feel the same.

—Talbot Davis
Lead Pastor, Good Shepherd Church

This is a profound work. For far too long, our understanding of holiness has been truncated. Matt O'Reilly has developed a work that stirs the reader to move from dull understandings of holiness into a fresh awakening to the fullness of life God has made available to every believer. Whether you are a layperson, a clergyperson, or a professor in a seminary, this is a must read!

—Paul Lawler
Lead Pastor, Christ Church Memphis

The doctrine of sanctification is both vitally important and widely neglected in much of contemporary Christianity. Matt O'Reilly offers a study of the doctrine that is not only helpful but also eminently readable and delightful. This book will be a blessing to pastors, teachers, Bible study groups, and earnest Christians everywhere.

—Thomas H. McCall
Timothy C. and Julie M. Tennent Professor of
Theology, Asbury Theological Seminary

Holiness is at the core of our Wesleyan faith and way, yet it has been given far too little attention. I joyfully welcome this book. I not only affirm it, I urge you to read and appropriate its message; pass it along for another to read.

—Maxie Dunnam
Pastor-at-Large, Christ Church Memphis

I rejoiced when I read Matt O'Reilly's *Free to Be Holy*. Matt powerfully connects holiness and mission. His assertion that our lives always tell some story about our God is spot on. I strongly encourage Christians of all stripes to read this book and commit themselves anew to telling the truth about God's character with the character of their lives.

—Kimberly D. Reisman
Executive Director, World Methodist Evangelism

As a central feature of the Christian life, holiness is underreported. But as Matt so rightly says, "[God] wants a people who embody his holy character so that they can represent him well and truthfully to all the families of the earth." I'm grateful for this tour that follows the thread of holiness through Scripture, from cover to cover, to inspire us all toward the good life.

—Carolyn Moore
Host of the Art of Holiness podcast

Writing in clear and engaging language, Dr. O'Reilly explores eight biblical passages that clearly establish both the need and the possibility of holy living. With his sound exegesis, he is able to avoid abstract theologizing, making the concepts clear and appealing. This will be a helpful book to put in the hands both of the nominal Christian who does not recognize the possibility and the earnest Christian who wants to go deeper but does not know how. Warmly recommended.

—John N. Oswalt
Visiting Distinguished Professor of Old
Testament, Asbury Theological Seminary

Matt O'Reilly offers a coherent, compelling, and accessible explanation of the doctrine of holiness in *Free to Be Holy*. O'Reilly's work will help the church to recover the rest of the gospel message—not only freedom from the guilt of sin but also freedom from the power of sin so that believers can reflect holiness in this life as God intended. O'Reilly declares the good news that perfect love for God and neighbor is possible through union with Christ and continual walking in the Spirit.

—Suzanne Nicholson
Professor of New Testament, Asbury University

Matt O'Reilly has given us a clear, accessible, and biblical guide to the meaning of holiness and how to live a holy life. This book is a great resource for clergy and laity alike. Highly recommended!

—David Watson
Dean, United Theological Seminary

FREE TO BE HOLY

A BIBLICAL THEOLOGY OF SANCTIFICATION

MATT O'REILLY

Copyright 2024 by Matt O'Reilly

All rights reserved. No part of this publication may be reproduced, stored in a retrieval system, or transmitted, in any form or by any means—electronic, mechanical, photocopying, recording, or otherwise—without prior written permission, except for brief quotations in critical reviews or articles.

Unless otherwise noted, Scripture quotations are from the New Revised Standard Version Bible, copyright © 1989 National Council of the Churches of Christ in the United States of America. Used by permission. All rights reserved.

Scripture quotations marked ESV are from the The Holy Bible, English Standard Version®, copyright © 2001 by Crossway, a publishing ministry of Good News Publishers. Used by permission. All rights reserved.

Scripture quotations marked NIV are taken from the Holy Bible, New International Version®, NIV® Copyright © 1973, 1978, 1984, 2011 by Biblica, Inc.™ Used by permission of Zondervan. All rights reserved worldwide. www.zondervan.com. The "NIV" and "New International Version" are trademarks registered in the United States Patent and Trademark Office by Biblica, Inc.™ All rights reserved worldwide.

Scripture quotations marked NASB are taken from the New American Standard Bible®. Copyright © 1960, 1962, 1968, 1971, 1972, 1973, 1975, 1977, 1995 by The Lockman Foundation. Used by permission.

Printed in the United States of America

Page design and layout by PerfecType, Nashville, Tennessee

O'Reilly, Matt, Dr.
Free to be holy : a Biblical theology of sanctification / Matt O'Reilly. - Franklin, Tennessee : Seedbed Publishing, ©2024.

    pages ; cm.

    ISBN: 9798888000793 (paperback)
    ISBN: 9798888000809 (epub)
    ISBN: 9798888000816 (pdf)
    ISBN: 9798888000823 (DVD)
    OCLC: 1443742416

    1. Sanctification--Christianity. 2. Holiness--Christianity. 3. Love--Biblical teaching. 4. Theological anthropology--Christianity. I. Title.

BT765.O73 2024   234/.8   2024941415

SEEDBED PUBLISHING
Franklin, Tennessee
seedbed.com

To Walter Albritton, my pastor, friend,
and father in the faith

CONTENTS

Foreword	xi
Acknowledgments	xv
Introduction	1
1. Our Purpose and Our Problem (Genesis 1–3)	5
2. What Does God Want? (Exodus 19)	19
3. Everything Is Yes (Isaiah 6)	33
4. How Will God Get What He Wants? (Ezekiel 36)	45
5. Is Perfect Love Possible? (Matthew 5)	59
6. Free to Be Fully Human (Romans)	73
7. What Is God's Will for Me? (1 Thessalonians and Philippians)	87
8. Why Did Jesus Come? (1 John)	101
Conclusion	113
An Invitation to Awakening	123
About Seedbed	127

FOREWORD

Christianity is all about holiness. We Jesus-followers need to always remember and focus on our Lord's conversation recorded in Matthew 22:37–40. When asked about the most important commandment he said, "'You shall love the Lord your God with all your heart and with all your soul and with all your mind.' This is the greatest and first commandment. And a second is like it: 'You shall love your neighbor as yourself.' On these two commandments hang all the law and the prophets."

Jesus did not just name the two commandments, he said that the entire Bible of his day hangs on those two. The New Testament calls this obedience of love "sanctification" and says that it is God's will for our lives (1 Thess. 4:3). The Bible teaches how people should become more and more holy in obedience to Jesus's command in the Sermon on the Mount, "Be perfect, therefore, as your heavenly Father is perfect" (Matt. 5:48).

Since the beginning of the Methodist movement, Wesleyan Christians have focused on *scriptural* holiness. It is scriptural because we believe that the whole Bible teaches this way of salvation. John Wesley said that this way of salvation is the general tenor—the whole theme and content—of the Bible. He also said that all of our biblical interpretation should be done with reference to this "grand scheme of doctrine" that runs through the whole Bible (*Explanatory Notes on the New Testament*; Romans 12:6). By this we mean that God's grace is at work in our lives bringing forth repentance, justification, and sanctification. We are saved by grace through faith (Eph. 2:8–10).

While many believe in scriptural holiness, too often it is talked about without specific descriptions of how the whole Bible points toward holiness. Too often Christians focus on one book or one part of the Bible. In *Free to Be Holy*, Matt O'Reilly shows how sanctification—the goal of the Christian life—is based on the entire Bible. He brings together Old Testament stories as well as New Testament teachings. By the end of the book, readers will see how the theme of holiness ties all of Scripture together.

He closes each chapter with questions for reflection that bring the Bible's message home in very practical ways. It is not enough to see the general tenor of Scripture. We must understand how it impacts our relationship with Christ and how God's calling on our lives can lead us day by day.

I have been told by those outside our movement that it is God's calling for Wesleyans to emphasize sanctification and help the whole Christian church in all denominations to reclaim this basic teaching of the faith. This book is a significant response to that calling.

Scott J. Jones
Bishop, Global Methodist Church
June 27, 2024

ACKNOWLEDGMENTS

No book is the work of the author alone, and I am indebted to many for their support in the writing of this one. In particular, I am inexpressibly grateful to my friend of more than twenty years, Jay Arnold, who read and provided substantive feedback on more than a few pages of this manuscript. He has always encouraged me to write and to write well, and for that I give thanks and continue to strive to do so. To be sure, any remaining shortcomings in my work are not for lack of a devoted friend who is also a gifted editor. I give thanks also for my wife, Naomi, and our children, who have lovingly supported my writing, especially given that time in the study is not time with them. The team at Seedbed has been spectacular in their support of this second project, especially my editor, Andrew Dragos, who has provided crucial feedback with unfailing patience. The congregations of Hope Hull Community Church and

Christ Church Birmingham have been deeply supportive of my writing, a posture I do not take for granted. I owe much to the many with whom I've had long discussions on the question of holiness over the years, not least Walter Albritton, Allan Coppedge, John Oswalt, Billy Coppedge, and Isaac Hopper. Their influence will be perceptible by those who know them. In addition, this book is the fruit of countless other conversations with the members and staffs of the churches I've served, my students who engaged the material in the context of the classroom, members of the St. Peter Fellowship of the Center for Pastor Theologians, members of the Francis Asbury Society Holiness Collaborative, and my faculty colleagues at Wesley Biblical Seminary. I owe much to all of them. Finally, I am grateful to you, the reader, and my ongoing prayer for you is the prayer of the apostle: "May the God of peace himself sanctify you entirely; and may your spirit and soul and body be kept sound and blameless at the coming of our Lord Jesus Christ. The one who calls you is faithful, and he will do this" (1 Thess. 5:23–24).

INTRODUCTION

I distinctly remember thinking, *There must be more to Christianity than this*. I was a teenager. I was a Christian. And I was frustrated. I was frustrated because so much of Christian teaching focused on hope for the next life but had little to say regarding hope for this life. I've since learned what was happening to me. I was reacting to a form of American Christianity in which the gospel was all about God's forgiveness—freedom from guilt and condemnation—but very little was said about freedom from sin. In fact, the general assumption was that sin is just part of being human. You can't really be free from it. At least, not *completely* free. People stumble. There's not much to be done about it. So just grin and bear it and be grateful for God's mercy. And remember—Christians aren't perfect, just forgiven.

This widespread version of Christianity—offering heaven in the next life but not freedom from sin in this life, offering freedom from the consequences of sin but not from the power of sin—promises deliverance from guilt but not from the things that produce that guilt. Such a truncated gospel contains only half of the story. I've written this book about the rest of the gospel—the part we sometimes forget.

Now let me be clear: I'm not suggesting that forgiveness isn't part of the good news. To the contrary, forgiveness is foundational. It's essential. When Jesus gathered his followers for one last meal before going to the cross, he insisted that his coming death was for the forgiveness of sins (Matt. 26:28). The book of Acts tells us that the apostles repeatedly proclaimed the forgiveness of sins (Acts 2:38; 10:43; 13:38; 26:18). The apostle Paul insists that in Christ we have the forgiveness of sins (Eph. 1:7; Col. 1:14). There's no gospel without the good news that our sins are forgiven in Jesus. But that's not the whole story. There's more. Much more. While forgiveness is essential to the gospel, it's only *part* of the gospel. Sadly, much of the church has forgotten the rest. I've written this book to help us remember.

So if forgiveness is only part of the gospel, what's the rest of it? In short, the rest of the gospel consists of the good news that Jesus died and was raised to set us free, not only from the guilt of sin but also from its power. Jesus died so that we can be thoroughly transformed—so that we can consistently embody his character. In a word, the rest of the gospel is *holiness*.

This brings us to the question of holiness, and it turns out there are two. First, what is holiness? Second, how holy can we expect to be in this life? Now different people have different ideas about words like *holy* and *holiness*. For some, holiness smacks of legalism. They think of it in terms of rules: if you keep the rules, you're holy; if you don't, you're not. That's not what I mean by holiness. For others, holiness refers exclusively to an attribute of God that we don't share. God is holy, but we're not, and we never can be. That's not what I mean either.

As you work through this book, the thing that will keep coming up is this: when human beings are holy, they embody the character of God. Think about it like this: God always does what's right. He always does what he *ought* to do. For us, then, to be holy is to be formed in such a way that we consistently do what we *ought* to do—like God does. And when our lives are transformed in this way, our words and our actions consistently tell the truth about God and his character. Don't you want your life to tell the truth about God's character? I sure do. I want that for both of us.

1
Our Purpose and Our Problem

Genesis 1–3

> *Then God said, "Let us make humankind in our image, according to our likeness; and let them have dominion over the fish of the sea, and over the birds of the air, and over the cattle, and over all the wild animals of the earth, and over every creeping thing that creeps upon the earth."*
>
> *So God created humankind in his image,*
>   *in the image of God he created them;*
>   *male and female he created them.*
>
> *God blessed them, and God said to them, "Be fruitful and multiply, and fill the earth and subdue it; and have dominion over the fish of the sea and over the birds of the air and over every living thing that moves upon the earth."*

> *God said, "See, I have given you every plant yielding seed that is upon the face of all the earth, and every tree with seed in its fruit; you shall have them for food."*
>
> —Genesis 1:26–29

It may seem strange to begin this study in Genesis. After all, this book is about holiness, and the word *holy* only appears once in all of Genesis (2:3). And the one time it shows up, it doesn't refer to God or to us. Holiness language doesn't become prominent in the biblical story until halfway through Exodus. So why start with Genesis? Here's the reason: the opening chapters of Genesis are crucial for understanding what it means to be human. And while holiness is one of the chief ways to speak of God, holiness is also very much about experiencing human life in its fullness. Holiness is about God's best for us. And if we skip the opening chapters of the story, our vision of God's design for human life will be deeply impoverished. Genesis introduces themes that will show up again and again as we work through the passages on holiness under consideration in this study. Reading Genesis as a foundation for our study of holiness reminds us that many passages in the Bible deal with holiness without ever mentioning the word *holy*. Concepts that inform our understanding of holiness are often present even when the word is not explicitly stated.

In short, if we want to get the question of holiness right, we need to start with Genesis.

God's Image and Our Purpose

When you read Genesis, you find out right away that people matter to God. That's the climactic point of the creation story in Genesis 1, and it's a point that's made in several ways. Consider first how the creation of human beings breaks the repetition that marks the story of the days of creation. "And God said, 'Let there be . . . And it was so. . . . And there was evening and there was morning . . .'" That pattern shows up seven times with little variation in Genesis 1:1–25. It's repetitive. It's predictable. You know it's coming. But suddenly in verse 26, God says something else. Instead of, "Let there be," God says, "Let us make . . ." In every instance up to this point he creates almost casually. Light, sky, earth, stars, trees, fish, birds, everything—he calls for them, and they come into being. But here God doesn't simply call human beings into existence. He pauses. He reflects. He considers the nature and the purpose of his next creative act. That shift—the shift from creative speech to reflective speech—signals a change that calls for the reader to pay attention. It means that the next thing God will make is unlike anything he's made up to that point.

The second signal that human beings are the unique climax of God's creative work comes in the content of his reflective speech. Here God reveals his special plan for humanity. Human beings will carry God's image. This means that every human being—regardless of ethnicity, age, sex, or anything else—is made in the image of God. We've all heard this, but what does it mean and why does it matter? Take a moment to consider how images work. If you were to walk into a pagan temple in the ancient world, you would see a statue of the deity to whom the temple was devoted. That statue—that *image*—represents the presence of the deity. Ancient peoples even had rituals they performed on the eyes and mouth of the statues to activate their representative function. These rituals reveal that the statue wasn't merely a stand-in for the deity. To the contrary, the statue represented the very presence of the deity. Similarly, if you were a king in the ancient world, there would likely be statues of you set up around your kingdom. You may have put them up yourself, or someone else may have erected them as a way of honoring you. Either way, each statue serves as a constant reminder to everyone who sees it that you're the king. It represents your authority. It represents you.

Perhaps this helps us see the significance of being made in God's image. God made us to represent him—to embody his character and live in ways that reflect the beauty of his glory throughout creation. This also means that every human being has inherent dignity. You were made to represent the one true God, the God who made all things. That means that you matter. And it means that God has placed a great deal of trust in you. In fact, he's entrusted you with his reputation. Now this implies a grave responsibility. If you and I don't live to honor God, it doesn't mean we're no longer representing him. Instead, it means that we're falsely representing him. That, of course, is precisely what happens as the story of Genesis proceeds. A couple of chapters later, we read about Adam's rebellion. Adam didn't stop representing God when he rebelled. He was still made in God's image. He didn't lose that. But he did deform the image of God in himself. With Adam's sin, the image of God that all of us carry was damaged. And our natural ability to represent him well was damaged too. The whole story of the Bible is about what God will do to repair his image in us. If you're interested in knowing what Genesis has to do with holiness, here's a hint: holiness is about embodying the image of God and doing it well. Holiness is about representing God as he ought to be represented. That's his purpose for you and me.

God's Image and Our Character

If you and I are to represent God the way he ought to be represented, then our character must correspond to his character. And while this carries implications for our behavior, it's far deeper than mere behavior. The point is that if I'm to represent God well, then I must *become* a certain kind of person. Once I become that sort of person, then I'll also behave in a way that honors God.

This emerges in Genesis 2:15–17 with the command not to eat the fruit from the tree of the knowledge of good and evil. Now this passage is easily misunderstood. People often wonder why God would issue such a command knowing its violation would unleash unimaginable evil and suffering into the world. Why should all that wickedness—all that pain!—result from one bite into that one piece of fruit? But that's the point. It wasn't just a piece of fruit. The tree of the knowledge of good and evil presented Adam with the opportunity to live in a way that honored God, to be a person of integrity, and to willingly do good and avoid evil. And apart from the commandment to avoid the fruit of a single tree, there's no way to talk about integrity. There's no other way to speak of right and wrong. There's no other way to begin thinking of holiness.

Pay attention to how the command also reveals something about God's character. We often focus on the one tree that God forbids. But before forbidding Adam to eat from the one tree, God told him, "You may freely eat of every tree of the garden" (Gen. 2:16). This displays God's unmatched generosity. The text frames the whole encounter in light of God's abundant provision. But we tend to focus on that one tree—the one Adam *can't* have—instead of all the other trees that he *can*.

Imagine that I offered to give you everything I own. You could enjoy it, care for it, and make use of it. The only stipulation is that I want to keep one thing for myself. It's a pocket watch, and it belonged to my dad. It's special to me. You can have everything but that. How would you respond? You would likely respond with profound gratitude, praising my generosity and telling others how kind I'd been to you. Never mind one old watch when you can have everything else. You would focus on what I'd *given* you, not on what I'd *kept* from you. And if you did happen to tell someone how I'd stingily kept one thing for myself, you'd appear remarkably ungrateful.

So why do we focus on the one thing God withheld from Adam when we ought to celebrate the generosity God displayed by giving Adam so much? We ought to see the whole scene as an opportunity for Adam to honor God with grateful obedience. After all, that's what he should've done. Do you see how framing the tree and the fruit this way turns our attention to Adam's character? The tree of the knowledge of good and evil puts Adam in a position to become the kind of person who gives himself completely to God in love. But for that to be a real option, another option has to be possible too. Adam must also have the option of turning his heart away from God. And that's exactly what happened. Instead of allowing his character to be formed in holiness, Adam allowed his character to be deformed by sin. It's always one or the other. Either we offer ourselves to God and receive his best or we turn from God and lose the good things he offers to us. That's what happened to Adam. He insisted on eating from the one forbidden tree and was consequently exiled from the garden. That means he also lost all the other trees that God had given him. "You may freely eat of every tree in the garden"—that's hard to do when the garden is no longer your home.

God's Mission and Our Holiness

Adam was never supposed to be exiled from the garden, but he *was* always supposed to leave it. Remember that first command, "Be fruitful and multiply, and *fill the earth* and subdue it" (Gen. 1:28, italics added). God always intended for Adam and his children to go out from the garden on a mission to carry God's just, loving, and holy rule to the whole planet. That's what it means to be God's representatives. That's God's mission for his human creatures. But when Adam sinned, he severely hindered the mission. And when he left the garden, he left under God's judgment rather than with God's blessing.

We need to understand the relationship between holiness and mission. This will come up more than once as we work our way through this study. To depart from the garden in faithful mission under God's global mandate, Adam needed to maintain his relationship with God. He needed to be holy. But when Adam sinned against God, he ruptured his relationship with God, forfeiting his commission and undercutting his objective. His sin stood in the way of his missional purpose.

As this book continues, I hope it becomes clear that holiness is crucial for maximizing missional effectiveness. It's stunningly difficult—perhaps impossible—to fulfil the mission God has entrusted to us if we disregard God's desire that we become holy. If God desires to have a world full of people who embody his character, then the spread of holiness is the mission of the church. Allow this dynamic to frame the way you see the work of Jesus on our behalf. Jesus came to reconcile us to God and bring us back into fellowship with his Father and ours. To accomplish that, our sin had to be dealt with. It had to be forgiven. But forgiveness of sin isn't the ultimate goal. It's the necessary first step to making us holy so that we can fulfill our missional purpose, which is to fill the earth with disciples who embody the beauty of the character of the triune God. That mission hasn't changed. It remains consistent throughout Scripture. That's why the prophets declare, "the earth will be filled with the knowledge of the glory of the Lord, as the waters cover the sea" (Hab. 2:14). That means that the day will come when the earth will be as full of the glory of God as the Atlantic Ocean is with water. When will that be? And how does it happen? The earth will be filled with the knowledge of God's glory when it's filled with people who embody God's character. That's our mission. Adam may have failed, but Jesus succeeded. He died and was raised to make us holy so that we can fulfill that very mission.

Who Gets to Be God?

If we're reading the creation account through the lens of *holiness*, then another question comes up: namely, the question of authority. Who gets to be God? We've already noticed that Adam had been given significant authority—*global authority*. But his authority wasn't unlimited, and it did not originate in him. Instead, it was a gift. It came to him from God. And that made Adam's authority different from God's authority. God's authority is universal; Adam's authority, though significant, was limited. God's authority originates from his nature; Adam's authority was delegated to him by God. The command not to eat from that one tree was to serve as a constant reminder of this. It was to serve as a reminder of the limits of Adam's authority, which was never absolute.

So when Adam ate the forbidden fruit, he went beyond the bounds of his authority. His action said to God, "I don't acknowledge your authority. I insist on being my own authority. I insist on my own absolute and universal rule. And I don't care what you think about it." Adam took for himself the authority that belonged God. There's another name for attitudes and behaviors that take what rightfully belongs to God only to offer it to someone or something else. It's called idolatry. At its root, Adam's sin was idolatry. By refusing to obey God, he refused to worship God. He insisted on elevating himself, his preferences, and his desires. All of that should open our eyes to the relationship between holiness and worship. False worship (or idolatry) corrupts holiness, undermines it, and darkens it. In contrast, true worship cultivates holiness. Once again, we'll see this relationship come up elsewhere in the Bible. For now, let's understand that apart from the true worship of the one true God, there is no holiness.

From Worship to Holiness to Mission

Let's conclude this introductory chapter by restating this foundational claim. True worship cultivates the holiness necessary for faithful mission. If Adam had allowed God to remain as the highest authority, worshipping God and obeying him, then Adam would have continued growing in holiness, and he would have left the garden with God's favor to rule the whole earth as God's representative. But he didn't. He became idolatrous. Refusing to give God the worship that only God deserves, Adam fell from holiness into sin, and with the image of God in him damaged, he left the garden, not on a mission to fill the world with the beauty of the rule of God, but under God's condemnation. These three things belong together: worship, holiness, and mission. If we lose any one of them, we are in danger of losing all three.

Questions for Reflection and Discussion

1. What was your understanding of holiness before beginning this study?

2. Have you ever met anyone who seemed particularly holy to you? What made them seem that way?

3. What aspects of God's character are revealed in the creation narrative of Genesis 1–2?

4. Does the statement "Worship cultivates holiness" impact your attitude toward the importance of worship in your local church?

5. What are some specific ways you can become more involved in the church's mission?

2

What Does God Want?

Exodus 19

> *Then Moses went up to God; the LORD called to him from the mountain, saying, "Thus you shall say to the house of Jacob, and tell the Israelites: You have seen what I did to the Egyptians, and how I bore you on eagles' wings and brought you to myself. Now therefore, if you obey my voice and keep my covenant, you shall be my treasured possession out of all the peoples. Indeed, the whole earth is mine, but you shall be for me a priestly kingdom and a holy nation. These are the words that you shall speak to the Israelites."*
>
> —Exodus 19:3–6

Relationships come with expectations. That's easy to see. For example, when two people commit to marriage, they bring expectations. A wife and a husband both expect the other to be exclusively and unconditionally committed. We expect parents to nurture and care for their children. Employees are expected to offer their best to an employer. And employers are expected to look out for the interests of their employees. Such expectations aren't always met, of course. And when they aren't, we may feel a range of emotions from disappointment to betrayal. Expectations for conduct are essential to every relationship. It's no different in our relationship with God.

What Does God Want?

So if we're interested in any sort of relationship with God, we should also be interested in what God expects for that relationship. And that is precisely the question that comes up in the opening verses of Exodus 19: What does God want from his people? That question will go on to occupy much of what follows, not only in Exodus, but throughout the whole Bible.

As Exodus 19 begins, the Hebrew people find themselves at the foot of Mt. Sinai. At this point in the narrative, they've been through a lot. The story of their journey into Egypt comes near the end of Genesis (45–46) when they were a much smaller in number. Jacob (Abraham's grandson) and his family moved to Egypt, where he was reunited with his son Joseph, whom Jacob had thought was dead. Joseph had actually been sold into slavery years before by his jealous brothers, who led their father to believe his beloved Joseph was dead. By means of God's providence, Joseph came to Egypt and ascended to a place of great authority, second only to Pharaoh. When Joseph's brothers came to Egypt seeking relief from a famine, he orchestrated a plan to have them bring his father. To make a long story short, Joseph forgave his brothers for their sin against him, and Genesis ends with Jacob's whole family reconciled and settled in Egypt.

The story goes south from there. The book of Exodus begins with news that a new Pharaoh had ascended to the throne of Egypt. This ruler had no regard for Joseph and was afraid of how numerous the Hebrew people had become. He feared war with them (Ex. 1:8–10). To avoid that, this new Pharaoh enslaved the Hebrews and forced them to work under grueling and oppressive conditions. As things grew worse, they cried out to God for rescue (Ex. 2:23–25). And God acted. He called a man named Moses to represent him before Pharaoh. God instructed Moses to tell Pharaoh to free the Hebrew people. Despite his initial reluctance, Moses finally obeyed. He went to Pharaoh and commanded him to release God's people. You won't be surprised to learn that Pharaoh didn't receive this command well. He refused to obey it, and the consequences came in the form of ten devastating plagues, culminating with the death of the firstborn sons in all of Egypt. After this, Pharaoh released the Hebrew people. But changing his mind, he foolishly pursued them and met his end in the waters of the Red Sea (Exodus 14). From there, God cared for his people in the wilderness (despite their grumbling!) and took them to the foot of Mt. Sinai, where he established them as a nation and gave them his covenant. That brings us to Exodus 19.

Covenant and Holiness

A covenant is a kind of relationship. In the ancient world, a covenant was often used to bind a king to a people. Like all relationships, covenants came with expectations. The king would provide protection, and the people would pay him tribute of one sort or another. The notion of covenant is important for our study because the covenant provides the crucial context for understanding holiness in the Bible. Remember that the word *holy* appears only once in Genesis, and prior to Mt. Sinai, it appears only a few times in Exodus. From this point forward, however, with the giving of the covenant, holiness language becomes much more frequent. In fact, it becomes a major theme. We've already anticipated the reason, but I'll restate it for the sake of clarity. A covenant is a relationship, and, like all relationships, covenants have expectations. The word for the expectations that come with this covenant is *holiness*.

God introduces the covenant expectations by reminding the people how much they mean to him and what he's done for them. He emphasizes how he rescued them in stunning displays of his power and "bore you on eagles' wings and brought you to myself" (Ex. 19:4). He treasures them and has chosen them from among all the nations to be his special people. But if they're to have this relationship, they have to obey him. They must keep the covenant (19:5). After all, relationships have expectations. Here we discover what God expects, and it's articulated in two related but distinct ways. God expects them to be (1) a "priestly kingdom" and (2) a "holy nation." Let's take those two in turn.

Priestly Kingdom

God's first expectation is that his people be a kingdom of priests. Yes, he's going to give them a special group of priests to care for the tabernacle (and later the temple). But the fact that they have priests doesn't negate their calling to be a kingdom of priests. Perhaps we could call this dynamic *the priesthood of all Israelites*. But what does that calling involve? What precisely does all this mean? Well, it helps to think about what a priest does. The key idea is that priests function as mediators. They stand between God and the people. And from that middle place, they represent God to the people and the people to God. If an Israelite needed to make an offering, the priest would oversee the process, ensuring it's done in a way that honors God. And if it is, the priest is authorized to address the worshipper on God's behalf and say that the worshipper's sins are forgiven and that God accepts their sacrifice.

To understand the calling to be a kingdom of priests, we need to apply that mediatorial role to the nation as a whole. But which parties does the nation as a whole mediate between? The answer comes in Exodus 19:6: God indicates that he has chosen the Hebrew people from among all the *other* peoples. In the same breath, he reminds them that the whole earth belongs to him. God could have chosen any nation he wanted, but he looked at all the nations and chose *this specific* nation for a special priestly vocation to be his representatives. To whom? To all the other nations that weren't chosen for this vocation. God has chosen them to stand between him and the other nations to show those nations what God is like. That's what it means to be a kingdom of priests.

Now this shouldn't come as too big of a surprise. After all, when God called Abraham, he promised that Abraham's family would be his instrument to bless all the families of the earth (Gen. 12:3). God's desire is not to pick a single family for himself so that they can be his alone with everyone else left out. His desire has always been to bless every tribe, every ethnicity, and every people group. He picked one family—Abraham's family—to be his special possession so that they might convey his blessing to all other families and nations. Israel's calling to be a priestly kingdom in Exodus 19 represents God's plan for keeping his promise to Abraham. They'll be God's priests to the nations because God wants to bless the nations.

The expectation that God's people will act as his representatives shows up again in the second commandment of the Ten Commandments. The first commandment requires that the people worship God alone, which means they shall not make or worship idols. The second command is one that many remember: "You shall not take the name of the LORD your God in vain" (Ex. 20:7 ESV). Most people assume this means they shouldn't attach the word *god* to profanity (or swear words). But a closer look reveals that there's much more going on here. Exodus was originally written in Hebrew, and the Hebrew word here translated *take* also means "to lift" or "to carry" or "to bear." That same word shows up later in Exodus 28:29 in a description of the breastplate of the high priest. The high priest had very specific clothes to wear when he ministered before God, and part of his clothing was a breastplate covered with twelve very precious stones. The stones represented the twelve tribes of Israel. And by wearing this piece of clothing, the high priest was said to "*bear* the names of the sons of Israel . . . when he goes into the holy place, for a continual remembrance before the LORD" (Ex. 28:29, italics added). The word *bear* in this verse is the same word in Hebrew that is translated "take" in 20:7 (the commandment about God's name). In chapter 20, God tells the people about their priestly vocation and stipulates that they must not *bear* his name in vain. In chapter 28, the high priest is told that part of his vocation is to *bear* the names of the twelve tribes before God. Both passages reveal what it means to be a priest—whether that's a specific high priest or the priestly nation as a whole. That topical similarity suggests "take" (20:7) and "bear" (28:29) likely mean the same thing. God isn't simply telling his people not to attach his name to profanity (though of course they shouldn't do that). Rather, he's telling his people that by bearing his name they represent him. Not bearing God's name in vain means they must not misrepresent him. They must not represent him in a way that miscommunicates what he's like.[1] To be a priestly kingdom is to represent God, and he expects his people to represent him well.

---

1. For more on how the priestly garments provide context for what it means to bear God's name, see Carmen Joy Imes, *Bearing God's Name: Why Sinai Still Matters* (Downers Grove, IL: IVP Academic, 2019), 48–52.

Did you notice also how the first two commandments involve the worship of God and the people's vocation to represent God? Just as in Genesis, true worship is the foundation of representing God well. You won't be surprised that we now come to the question of holiness.

Holy Nation

What does it look like to represent God well? That question brings us to the second dynamic of God's plan for his people. God's people are called to be a *holy nation*. To flesh this out, we're going to step over to Leviticus—the next book in the Old Testament. Leviticus contains a major section known as *the holiness code* (Leviticus 17–27). This section is called the holiness code because the word *holy* recurs frequently. We're not going to look at the whole code. Instead, we're going to consider a few verses in chapter 19.

Leviticus 19 starts with Moses receiving a message from God for the people. Here's the first thing Moses is told to say: "You shall be holy, for I the LORD your God am holy" (19:2). Now remember that we're trying to understand what it means for God's people to be a holy nation. This verse helps us understand this because it compares God's holiness with the holiness he expects of his people. The word *holy* describes something about God that he wants his people to have too. We don't know what this holiness is yet. We only know that it's the same holiness as the holiness of God. To find out what it is, we have to keep reading.

The rest of Leviticus 19 explains what God wants when he calls upon his people to be holy. The chapter is filled with a series of practical instructions about how to treat other people. We need to look at only a few instances to begin to see what it means to be holy. In 19:9–10, the people are told to leave some of their crops along the edge of their fields at harvest time. They shouldn't take all the grapes on the vine. Instead, they're to leave some for the poor and for foreigners traveling through their land. These instructions are then punctuated by the declaration: "I am the LORD your God" (19:10). That declaration recalls God's opening statement at the beginning of the chapter: God is holy, and his people must be holy. That means they must embody generosity to those in need by leaving food in their fields for the needy to harvest. The practice is intended to teach the people about the character of God. God is generous. He was generous to the Israelites when they were strangers in Egypt. Now they must show the same generosity to strangers in their land. That's what it means to be holy as God is holy.

Take a look at 19:13: "You shall not keep for yourself the wages of a laborer until morning." What does it mean to be holy? It means you pay your employees on payday. It means you keep your end of the bargain. It means you treat people the way they ought to be treated. This point comes through even more clearly in the next verse: "You shall not revile the deaf or put a stumbling block before the blind" (19:14). Sadly, people with handicaps or disadvantages are often the targets of other people's cruelty. In this verse, God declares that his people must not engage in that sort of behavior. So God commands: if you're going to be my people, don't make fun of people who can't hear and don't trip people who can't see. Because God is holy, he takes care of vulnerable people. Therefore, his people must do the same. Holiness is about what we have in common with God. It's about God's desire to share his character with us. This point is crucial if we're to embrace what the Bible says about holiness. The truth about the character of God is revealed by the character of the people of God. The word that defines God's character is *holy*. Therefore, God's people must also become holy.

Embodied Holiness

I hope you're beginning to see that holiness isn't hypothetical. It's not an abstract theological concept with little practical importance. It's not just another theory or philosophy. At its heart, holiness is about our relationship with God—a relationship in which we come to share God's character. And that participation in God's holy character allows us to fulfill his purpose for us, namely, to represent him to others as he ought to be represented. God has decided to make himself known to the nations of the world through his people. That's why he promised Abraham that he would bless the nations through Abraham's family. That's why he set the Hebrew people free from Egyptian slavery. And that's why he incorporates us into Abraham's family. This is his purpose for us. The only way God will be known is if his people embody his character. Don't miss that word—*embody*. This is what makes holiness practical. Everything we've discovered about holiness indicates that there is no holiness except embodied holiness. We can say we love Jesus all we want, but if our behavior doesn't *embody* that love in our relationships with others, then we've not understood God's best for us. Holiness isn't an internal disposition with no bearings on our external life. If we're to share God's character, that character must show up in our visible and exterior bodily life. And as we'll find out in the next chapter, if God's people don't share his character, then we're lying to the world.

Questions for Reflection and Discussion

1. How would you have defined holiness before reading this chapter? Do you think about holiness differently now? How has your understanding changed?

2. What does it mean to be a kingdom of priests? How can you embody the priestly vocation to help other people draw near to God?

3. Why is it crucial for God's people to share God's character? What is at stake?

4. How does testifying to God's character in our world make you feel? Burdened? Honored?

5. Are you ready to answer the call to a priestly vocation? Does anything stand in the way?

3

Everything Is Yes

Isaiah 6

> *In the year that King Uzziah died, I saw the Lord sitting on a throne, high and lofty; and the hem of his robe filled the temple. Seraphs were in attendance above him; each had six wings: with two they covered their faces, and with two they covered their feet, and with two they flew. And one called to another and said:*
>
> *"Holy, holy, holy is the LORD of hosts;*
> *the whole earth is full of his glory."*
>
> *The pivots on the thresholds shook at the voices of those who called, and the house filled with smoke. And I said: "Woe is me! I am lost, for I am a man of unclean lips, and I live among a people of unclean lips; yet my eyes have seen the King, the LORD of hosts!"*

> *Then one of the seraphs flew to me, holding a live coal that had been taken from the altar with a pair of tongs. The seraph touched my mouth with it and said: "Now that this has touched your lips, your guilt has departed and your sin is blotted out." Then I heard the voice of the Lord saying, "Whom shall I send, and who will go for us?" And I said, "Here am I; send me!"*
>
> —Isaiah 6:1–8

It's easy to forget the importance of relying on God when things are good. We have what we need. We're comfortable. Sure, the occasional challenge might arise, but overall things are alright. Trusting God to meet our needs may not be our default posture in such times. And when a season like that is disrupted by some unexpected event, it's easy to grow anxious. We haven't spent much time cultivating reliance on God. After all, we've had things under control. And now that things are spinning out of control, it's difficult to move seamlessly into a posture that we haven't been cultivating. The good news is that seasons of disruption provide time to reorient our posture. They can often be seasons in which God makes himself known in powerful and beautiful ways.

That's the sort of situation we find at the beginning of Isaiah 6. Under the reign of Uzziah, Judah flourished.

The kingdom was prosperous, and the people secure and happy. Uzziah had been a good king, but now Uzziah is dead, and it's easy to imagine the sense of uncertainty that spread across the nation. *Will we still flourish? Will we still be secure?* The people of Judah would be presented with an opportunity to refocus their trust in God. But for that to happen, Isaiah's individual experience of God would need to become the experience of the people as a whole.

A New Vision of God

Isaiah's vision starts with God sitting on a throne. Thrones symbolize kingly power, and we're meant to see the contrast between the now dead human king and the living divine king. And we're meant to ask, Who is the proper object of our trust? To emphasize the trustworthiness and power of God, his throne is described as "high and lofty." That might not strike us as initially significant. After all, aren't all thrones positioned head and shoulders above everyone else? But then Isaiah begins to describe just how high and just how lofty this particular throne is. He does that by pointing out that "the hem of his robe filled the temple." The point isn't really the size of the room. The point is that a building made by human hands can't contain Israel's God. His strength and power and glory extend far beyond the bounds of our imagination. His wisdom and honor and beauty exceed our ability to describe. If the hem of his robe towers above us, the magnitude of his majesty can't be grasped.

Beyond the sheer magnitude of Isaiah's vision of the divine king, God is attended by two creatures called "seraphs." The Hebrew word is *seraphim*, and it's one of those words that's difficult to translate into English, which is why most translations just leave some version of the Hebrew word. The word likely means "fiery ones."[2] Both seraphs are positioned in flight on either side of God, and both have faces, feet, and six wings. That's about all we get as far as physical description, but we're meant to see that these are some sort of angelic beings that minister alongside the throne of God. Beyond their striking appearance, they're also calling out to one another and saying, "Holy holy, holy is the LORD of hosts; the whole earth is full of his glory" (6:3). With the sound of their voices, the building shakes; with their fiery presence, it's filled with smoke (6:4). We shouldn't pass quickly over the words they speak to one another. Of all the things they could say about God, the thing they describe is his holiness. When Isaiah encounters God, God's holiness dominates the experience. And it's not just mentioned once or twice. Three times the *seraphim* cry out: this God is holy, holy, holy.

---

2. See John Oswalt, *The Book of Isaiah, Chapters 1–39* NICOT (Grand Rapids: Eerdmans, 1986), 179.

Take a moment to consider the scene. Isaiah is having a vision of God in the temple. And the vision of God he sees is bigger than his ability to describe. And as he sees this lofty divine king, he also perceives the presence of these two angelic creatures. They're on fire, they're flying, and they're shouting. And what are they shouting about? They're calling out to one another (and to Isaiah) about the perfect and unimpeachable holiness of the one who sits on the throne. The building is shaking and filled with smoke. It's easy to see why Isaiah responds the way he does. The scene astonishes and terrifies him. And Isaiah knows that he's in trouble: "Woe is me! I am lost, for I am a man of unclean lips . . . yet my eyes have seen the King" (6:5). Confronted with God's perfect holiness, Isaiah perceives the depth of his own uncleanness. His unclean lips represent his whole being. He feels the weight of conviction. Being himself a transgressor, he stands condemned.

Unmet Expectations

Isaiah probably expects to die, especially when one of the fiery ones starts toward him. He likely thinks the fire of God's holiness is about to burn him up, just as the fire on the altar burned the offerings that were placed on it. As the seraph approaches, Isaiah notices the tongs with which it has clasped a coal from the altar. (You know that if a flaming angel needs tongs to hold a piece of coal, then that coal is *hot*.) Imagine Isaiah's dread—his fear. The end has come. King Uzziah, whom he loved, is dead. With Isaiah standing under conviction before God, a burning, shouting angel is coming to finish him off. It's over.

But Isaiah was about to learn something about the character of God. He was about to learn something about holiness. The thing he would learn is that in this moment of great sorrow and hopelessness, of fear and dread, the Holy One wasn't there to bash him over the head or teach him a lesson or punish him. The Holy One didn't intend to destroy Isaiah that day; instead, God intended to heal him. Imagine the moment Isaiah heard the words of the angel, "Now that this has touched your lips, your guilt has departed and your sin is blotted out" (6:7). What? My guilt is *gone*? My sin is *forgiven*? Can it be? The angel has touched Isaiah's unclean lips with the burning coal, and Isaiah, who thought the fire of God's holiness was there to burn him up, realizes with astonishment that it was there to make him whole.

This matters for the way we perceive the character of God. In nearly two decades of pastoral ministry, I've met many people who think that God is waiting for them to mess up so that he can punish him. They walk on eggshells, constantly afraid of what God might do to them if they do something wrong. But God isn't like that. God isn't waiting for us to make a mistake so that he can smite us. That's not what holiness is about. God wants us to experience his best. And God wants to reproduce his character in us—his *holy* character. Consequently, he's remarkably patient and unspeakably kind. He wants to cleanse us, heal us, and make us whole. He wants us to flourish. Isaiah had to learn that there were things in his life that were keeping him from flourishing and becoming holy. And when he encountered God, God dealt with those things. God dealt with Isaiah's sin and guilt so that Isaiah could be completely set apart for the thing God would call him to do. If there's something here to discover, it's this: the Holy One is good and has good things in store for us. Getting clean may not be fun, but the cleansing process is necessary for us to experience God's goodness. His holiness and his goodness aren't in conflict. They're one and the same.

Completely?

You may have noticed that in the last section I said Isaiah's cleansing resulted in him being *completely* set apart for what God would call him to do. I wonder if that word *completely* stood out to you. Perhaps it did. Perhaps you thought, *Can we really be set apart completely? Is it okay to use that kind of language?* Those are great questions. Let's look a little further at Isaiah's story and see what we find.

Immediately after Isaiah is cleansed, he hears a voice. It's the voice of God, and God has a question: "Whom shall I send, and who will go for us?" And Isaiah responds without hesitation, "Here am I; send me!" (6:8). Here's what striking about that answer: Isaiah signs up to go without knowing any details about the assignment. Where will he be going? Will he go alone? Or is he to be part of team? Is there any training? How much does it cost? What's the compensation? Is there a benefits package? If things don't go well, who's responsible? Is it dangerous? Isaiah doesn't ask any of these questions. He simply offers to go. No questions, no conditions, no negotiation. Every corner of Isaiah's heart is filled with one big *yes* to God. He holds nothing back. And if he holds nothing back, that means Isaiah is completely set apart.

Consider what this *doesn't* mean. It doesn't mean Isaiah won't make mistakes. It doesn't mean he won't be tempted, or that he knows everything there is to know, or that he no longer has any shortcomings. You see, being completely surrendered to God doesn't mean there's no room for improvement. It just means that everything in our hearts is saying *yes* to God. If God asks for something, the answer is *yes*. That's why it's good and right to talk about being completely set apart or entirely sanctified. If our answer to God is always *yes* and we hold nothing back, then we've fully surrendered to God's purposes in our lives.

Once again, we find that worship, holiness, and mission are interwoven in the pages of Scripture. Isaiah's vision was set in the Jerusalem temple, the place of worship. In the midst of true and honest worship of the Holy One, Isaiah was cleansed from his sin. And being sanctified, he unconditionally committed himself to the mission God had for him. Holiness is grounded in worship and expressed in mission. That's true for Isaiah; it's true for you and me.

Not Just Isaiah

The beautiful thing about this story is that Isaiah's experience isn't meant for him alone. Remember how Isaiah cried out, "I am a man of unclean lips, and I live among a people of unclean lips" (6:5)? That confession comes with major implications. We've already seen how Isaiah's unclean lips were cleansed when they were touched by the coal from the altar. The text intends for us to understand that all the Judean people have lips like Isaiah. His lips are unclean, and so are theirs. But if God can touch Isaiah's lips and cleanse them such that Isaiah's heart is set apart completely to God, then God can do that for the whole nation. And if God can do it for all of them, then he can do it for all of us. Isaiah encountered a holy God, and he became a holy man. The same can be true for you and me.

Take a moment to consider the whole process. Isaiah found himself in a time of uncertainty. In that time of uncertainty, God made himself known to Isaiah in a new way, revealing himself as the Holy One. That revelation of God's holiness shed light on Isaiah's sinfulness. His heart was laid bare, and it terrified him. But he found that the Holy One was also good and kind and that God's fire, instead of destroying Isaiah, was sent to cleanse him and set him apart. Because of this cleansing, Isaiah held nothing back from God. That's what it means to be holy.

So if we're thinking about holiness, then Isaiah 6 fills in the picture significantly. What is holiness? Holiness is a what happens when God graciously cleanses the heart and sets it apart for him. How holy can we reasonably expect to be in this life? This episode from Isaiah's life paints a picture of thorough holiness in which everything in the heart is completely offered to God. And I can know that everything in my heart is completely offered to God, if I'm willing to say an unconditional *yes* to whatever he asks.

Perhaps, as you reflect on these things, God is opening your eyes to the beauty of his holiness. And perhaps you're finding that that the light of his perfect love is illumining areas of your life that aren't completely surrendered to him. You've held them back, but now you know it's time to offer them to God. It's time for God to have your whole heart—for everything in your heart to say *yes* to him.

Questions for Reflection and Discussion

1. Do you remember a time in your life in which you experienced a major disruption? How did you experience God in the midst of that disruption? What did you learn about God's character?

2. Consider the suggestion that some people see God as someone who is waiting to punish them if they make a mistake. Have you ever thought about God this way?

3. What are the main images that come to mind when you think about God? Describe them as honestly and vividly as possible.

4. What does Isaiah's transformation reveal about God's character? What does it reveal about the work God wants to do in each of us?

5. It is said that we become what we worship. How would you assess this claim?

4

How Will God Get What He Wants?

Ezekiel 36

The word of the LORD came to me: Mortal, when the house of Israel lived on their own soil, they defiled it with their ways and their deeds; their conduct in my sight was like the uncleanness of a woman in her menstrual period. So I poured out my wrath upon them for the blood that they had shed upon the land, and for the idols with which they had defiled it. I scattered them among the nations, and they were dispersed through the countries; in accordance with their conduct and their deeds I judged them. But when they came to the nations, wherever they came, they profaned my holy name, in that it was said of them, "These are the people of the LORD, and yet they had to go out of his land." But I had concern for my holy name,

> *which the house of Israel had profaned among the nations to which they came.*
>
> *Therefore say to the house of Israel, Thus says the Lord God: It is not for your sake, O house of Israel, that I am about to act, but for the sake of my holy name, which you have profaned among the nations to which you came. I will sanctify my great name, which has been profaned among the nations, and which you have profaned among them; and the nations shall know that I am the Lord, says the Lord God, when through you I display my holiness before their eyes. I will take you from the nations, and gather you from all the countries, and bring you into your own land. I will sprinkle clean water upon you, and you shall be clean from all your uncleannesses, and from all your idols I will cleanse you. A new heart I will give you, and a new spirit I will put within you; and I will remove from your body the heart of stone and give you a heart of flesh. I will put my spirit within you, and make you follow my statutes and be careful to observe my ordinances.*
>
> —Ezekiel 36:16–27

You don't have to go to church long to discover that Christians can be sorted into one of two groups: those who don't like to talk about sin and those who do. Those who *do* are easy to identify because the sin they like to talk about isn't their own sin. It's yours. When it comes to those who *don't* like to talk about sin, there are two further categories. First, there are those who don't like to talk about sin and never do. When people sin, this group often ignores it or makes excuses for it. They dislike the awkwardness of talking about their transgressions, and they frequently soften the language of sin. I recently heard someone substitute "describing his flaws" for "confessing his sin." That indicates a person who doesn't want to use the "S-word." Second, there are those who don't like to talk about sin but are nevertheless willing to talk about it because they know that conviction and confession are essential to authentic forgiveness and healing. Ezekiel 36 gives an example of this. The prophet confronts the Hebrew people with the stark reality of their sin in order to draw them to repentance and assure them that God will wash them clean, not from *some* of their sin but from *all* of it.

Something Drastic

So far we've looked closely at what God wants for his people: he wants a people who embody his holy character so that they can represent him well and truthfully to all the families of the earth. Now it's time to consider a major barrier to our experience of God's best. In Ezekiel 36, the Hebrew people had to face the reality that their sin was keeping them from living out God's purposes for them as a people. Rather than representing him truthfully, they were misrepresenting him. Rather than being a blessing to all the families of the earth, they were dragging God's name through the mud by worshipping idols and committing murder. God is always true, but the sin of his people made him look untrue. God always does what's right, but the transgressions of his people made him out to be a wrongdoer. Despite this, God didn't give up on his people. He still desired to cleanse them and heal them and make them his faithful representatives. But before he could do that, he would have to do something to get their attention. Something big. Something drastic. Not because he didn't love them, but because he did. So what did he do? In 586 BC he allowed the Babylonians to come in and destroy Jerusalem and take her people into exile.

Ezekiel was a priest called upon to speak God's word to the people during this time of exile. Ezekiel explained that God had scattered the people because of their sin. They had sinned against one another, against the land, and against God. Ezekiel explains that they were called to sanctify God's name, given a vocation to show the world the beauty of the holiness of their God, and that they were supposed to do this by honoring him with their lives. In other words, by keeping God's law and thereby embodying his character. But instead of sanctifying God's name, they had profaned it. By disobeying God's commands, they had made him look powerless to save them. So God did something drastic to get their attention. He sent them into exile. He always planned to bring them back home, of course, but they had some things to learn first.

God's Concern for His Reputation

One thing they had to learn was how much God loves and esteems his name. Now that may strike some of us as strange. It may sound sort of prideful or egotistic. But God is neither of those things. In the ancient world, a person's name was deeply associated with their character. Think of the birth of Esau and Jacob narrated in Genesis 25. Jacob's name meant "he takes by the heel" or "he supplants" which is to take the place of another person through a scheme of some sort. And very quickly in the narrative, Jacob schemed and deceived in order to take Esau's birthright. His name told you about his character.

We don't connect a person's name and reputation today quite as closely as people did in the ancient world. Nevertheless, we do have some experience correlating a person's name and reputation. On one occasion during my college years, when my brother and I were visiting our grandmother, we made plans to meet some friends for dinner. As we were heading out, our grandmother handed us our coats and remarked, "Remember who you are." I'm not sure what she thought we might be getting into. It was an innocent dinner with friends. Whatever she thought, she was implying that the O'Reilly family had a good reputation in town, and she expected us not to tarnish it. In her mind, our family's name was associated with our family's reputation, and our behavior would either maintain a good reputation or tarnish it.

That's the sort of thing Ezekiel 36 means when it speaks of God's "concern for [his] holy name" (v. 21) and describes God's intention to act "for the sake of [his] holy name" (v. 22). God's name is associated with his character and his reputation, and since the Hebrew people carried his name with them, their character told a story about the character of their God. When God charges that "the house of Israel had profaned" his name among the nations (v. 21), the point is that they're misrepresenting his character. Their lives told a story about what their God was like. The problem was that the story they told with their lives was a lie. God's reputation was their responsibility, but they had betrayed that responsibility.

This resonates deeply with what we discovered in chapter 1 with Adam's story. Being made in the image of God, Adam was also a representative of God. And as long as he remained in relationship with God and honored God with his life, all would be well. His life would tell the truth about God's character and God's reputation would be safe. But as soon as Adam disobeyed, his life began to tell a lie about God, and he misrepresented God's character and sullied God's reputation. Adam's vocation to represent God wasn't put on hold when Adam sinned. It didn't go away. The image of God didn't suddenly vanish with Adam's transgression. No, Adam still stood as God's representative, but he began to represent God falsely. He profaned God's name. Upholding God's reputation was Adam's responsibility, and he failed. But Adam's failure doesn't determine the fate of the people of God. On the contrary, God is committed to enabling his people to represent him well. Which means he's committed to making them holy. That's what he wants. That's what he'll get. And that's what the rest of Ezekiel 36 is about.

Holiness Is the Mission

Before we consider how God intends to make his people holy, a major connection needs to be made, namely, the connection between holiness and mission. The connection comes in Ezekiel 36:23 when God speaks through Ezekiel and says, "the nations shall know that I am the Lord, says the Lord God, when through you I display my holiness before their eyes." This sheds significant light on God's purpose for his people. First, God wants the nations to know him. This echoes what we learned in Exodus 19 about the priestly vocation of the Hebrew people. Second, the way that the nations will come to know God is through the holiness of God's people. This clarifies the problem we've been exploring. If God is holy and if his people are to represent him well, then God's people must be holy too. When God's people embody his character as they represent him to the nations, the nations will come to know the character of God. The nations will see God's perfect love, consistent truth, and unwavering righteousness. This doesn't happen apart from the representative vocation of God's people. God, in his wisdom, has determined to make himself known through the character of human representatives. That means the mission of the people of God depends on the holiness of the people of God. If we become holy, the people we encounter will discover the beauty of the holiness of God. If we don't, they won't.

It should now be clear that our mission as God's people extends far beyond the initial experience of conversion. Unfortunately, that initial step is often the main and sometimes the only focus of our ministries. Of course, we want to see people convert to Jesus. That's crucially important. I certainly want to see people experience the life-giving love of Jesus. I want them to experience the forgiveness of sins.

I want to see people be reconciled to God. But that initial experience of reconciliation isn't the goal of our mission. Instead, it's a necessary first step. The goal of our mission is thoroughgoing transformation of the heart. We want people to experience forgiveness and to subsequently be made holy. That's what Ezekiel is describing. It starts with each of us and extends to our neighbors and the nations. God wants to make us holy. And when he does, all the families of the earth will be blessed as they come to know the Holy One.

How Will God Do It?

How will God create a holy people? How can sinners come to embody the character of God? The answer to these questions begins in Ezekiel 36:24. The Hebrew people are in exile. God allowed them to be taken out of their homeland by a foreign power as a consequence for their ongoing rebellion against his covenant. But now God will start the process of transformation by bringing them home: "I will take you from the nations, and gather you from all the countries, and bring you into your own land." Along with that, God declares that he will wash his people with clean water. God says that when he does that, "you shall be clean from all your uncleannesses, and from all your idols I will cleanse you" (36:25). Did you catch that? Not some of your uncleanness and idolatry. Not half of it. Not three-quarters of it. Not 99.99 percent of it. God declares that he will cleanse his people from *all* their uncleanness and from *all* their idolatry. That's the reason we're justified in speaking of *entire sanctification*. Sanctification is the process of being transformed such that we increasingly embody the character of God. What Ezekiel describes here goes far beyond initial forgiveness of sins and the judicial acquittal that comes at conversion. The prophet describes a real and thorough change. We are given a new heart and a new spirit. This transformation represents the continuing work of God after the initial experience of trusting him. If any part of us is left untouched by God's sanctifying power, then we're liable to misrepresent him, profaning his name and misleading others regarding the nature of his holy character. It's also crucial to note that God takes the responsibility for this work on himself. It's God—and God alone—who sanctifies his people. It's also God—and God alone—who cleanses us. Finally, it's God—and God alone—who takes away our idolatry. The work described in Ezekiel 36:25 is the work of God, and that means it's a work of grace. We can't accomplish our own sanctification, we can't cleanse ourselves, and we can't rid ourselves of idolatry. God must act. And he has.

Ezekiel continues to fill in the picture for us. God, as an act of his grace, will give his people new hearts, because the hearts we're born with are estranged from God and unreceptive to him. Ezekiel calls this "the heart of stone" (36:26). That was Israel's problem, and that's our problem. In their natural state, our hearts are hard and cold. They're unresponsive to God's voice and opposed to his lordship. The heart of stone serves as a metaphor for our resistance to God's loving rule in our lives. Like Adam's heart in the garden, our hard hearts insist on having our own way and being our own God. And there's nothing we can do in ourselves to change this. That's why God says, "*I will* remove from your body the heart of stone" (v. 26, italics added). Once again, when this happens, it's God who does it. Once again, that's what makes it grace. We don't get new hearts through our own strength or resources or intellect or power. God does the work. It's a gift.

Moreover, God insists that he will give his people a "new spirit"—his own Spirit—and in giving that new Spirit God will enable his people to obey him. Pay attention to that. The goal of God's transforming grace is to enable his people to *obey* him. God gives his Spirit to his people so that they can live in ways that honor him. God gives his Spirit so that we can be holy. That's how God gets what he wants.

Jesus and the Holy Spirit

Ezekiel 36 is what I like to call a text with a trajectory. This passage is going somewhere. It's pointing far beyond itself and far beyond the exile in which the Hebrew people found themselves when Ezekiel shared these words of hope. This passage is pointing to the coming of Jesus as well as to the coming of the Holy Spirit. With his death and resurrection, Jesus cleanses us from sin. He purchases our pardon. He offers us forgiveness. He takes our hearts of stone and gives us new hearts. We use all sorts of language to describe this initial experience of forgiveness and new life—conversion, justification, new birth. We cannot accomplish any of this ourselves. God himself must do the work of forgiveness for us and of regeneration in us. But remember, Ezekiel doesn't stop with the new heart. He continues by looking forward to the day when God's own Spirit would arrive and dwell within God's people. The day that Ezekiel was describing was the day of Pentecost narrated in Acts 2. The Spirit of God has come to the people of God. And having come, he is at work in each of us to enable us to embody God's holy character. The promises God made in Ezekiel 36 have been kept. That means the church has everything she needs for God to display his holiness in us before the nations. And as we increasingly embody God's holiness, the nations will know that our God is the one true God of perfect love. Holiness is the mission.

Questions for Reflection and Discussion

1. How do you understand the relationship between holiness and mission? Has your understanding of the mission of the church changed as you read this chapter? If so, how?

2. If Ezekiel 36 is looking forward to the coming of Jesus and the Holy Spirit, how does that impact your understanding of why Jesus and the Holy Spirit have come?

3. We might say that, in sending the Hebrew people into exile, God did something drastic to get their attention. What are some ways that God has worked to turn your attention to his purposes in your life?

4. Sometimes people find it hard to believe that God will cleanse them from *all* their sin. What are the barriers to believing that God's grace is powerful enough accomplish this thorough cleansing? Is there something in your life that makes it hard for you to believe God can sanctify you entirely?

5. Which people in your life need to see the beauty of God's character embodied in you? Will you be intentional in telling the truth about God with the way you live? What needs to change in your life for that to happen?

5
Is Perfect Love Possible?

Matthew 5

> *"You have heard that it was said, 'You shall love your neighbor and hate your enemy.' But I say to you, Love your enemies and pray for those who persecute you, so that you may be children of your Father in heaven; for he makes his sun rise on the evil and on the good, and sends rain on the righteous and on the unrighteous. For if you love those who love you, what reward do you have? Do not even the tax collectors do the same? And if you greet only your brothers and sisters, what more are you doing than others? Do not even the Gentiles do the same? Be perfect, therefore, as your heavenly Father is perfect."*
>
> —Matthew 5:43–48

Sometimes it's hard to take Jesus seriously. Most of us wouldn't want to admit that, but if we're honest, we'll recognize that it's true. Jesus's command to *be perfect* in Matthew 5:48 makes the point. Be perfect? As God the Father is perfect? Seriously? What is Jesus thinking? What does he expect? Everyone knows that no one is perfect. We remind ourselves of that frequently. Did Jesus miss the memo? Does he realize what he's saying? Is he exaggerating to make a point? Surely he means something else? After all, he couldn't really expect us to *be perfect*.

See how easy it is to take Jesus with less than full seriousness? We can come up with a thousand excuses for why Jesus didn't mean what he very clearly said. But what if he did intend to say exactly what he said? Take a moment and indulge me. What if this command from Jesus to *be perfect* is entirely serious? What if he means every syllable? And what if, in all our rationalizing, we are missing what he's actually saying? What if that means we're missing out on his best? What if we're actually missing out on a deep experience of God's own perfect love?

Can We Obey the Commands of Jesus?

Let's start with some questions. Does Jesus expect his commands to be obeyed? Do we have the ability to obey his commands? My answer to both of those question is *yes*.

For one, Matthew 28:19 instructs us to teach the nations to obey everything Jesus commanded. So the last words of Jesus recorded in the gospel of Matthew reiterate Jesus's own expectation that his commands are to be obeyed. Beyond that, it is the vocation of the church to teach obedience to the commands of Jesus. All this together indicates that Jesus fully expects his instruction to be obeyed and that implies that we are able (with the help of the Holy Spirit!) to actually obey the commands of our Lord. When Jesus offers an imperative, he's not just wasting his breath on some impossible standard that he doesn't expect us to embody. To the contrary, the commands of Jesus are real commands. The commands of Jesus are intended to be obeyed. The commands of Jesus can be realized in our lives, and not only ours but also the lives of the people of every nation. So we have two basic convictions. First, Jesus gives commands with the expectation that we obey. Second, Jesus enables us to obey his commands.

What Does It Mean to Be Perfect?

But that leaves us with another question. What does the command to *be perfect* mean in Matthew 5:48? To answer that question, we'll have to look closely at the context of the command. For starters, the command to "be perfect" is part of Jesus's Sermon on the Mount. More specifically, it forms the climax of a passage in which Jesus teaches on and intensifies several Old Testament laws and some ethical convictions of the time. Before clarifying these commands, Jesus calls for his followers to live in righteousness (v. 20). What does that mean? It means it's not enough to avoid something like murder if we harbor unrighteous anger in our hearts (vv. 21–22). It's not enough to avoid adultery if our hearts are filled with lustful desires (vv. 27–28). Jesus recognizes that divorce happens sometimes, but he rejects divorce generally, except in certain cases, because people are not meant to be used and then discarded (vv. 31–32). In these instances and others, instead of relaxing the commands of God, Jesus intensifies them by moving past the outward sinful behavior to the inward posture of our hearts that is the real source of sin.

Then in 5:43, Jesus says, "You have heard that it was said, 'You shall love your neighbor and hate your enemy.'" Unlike some of the other scriptural teachings Jesus develops, this saying isn't in the Old Testament. It's not one of God's commands to the Hebrew people. Perhaps it was conventional wisdom taught by some in the first-century Jewish world. Whatever the source, Jesus doesn't like it, and insists instead that his followers love their enemies and pray for their persecutors (v. 44). The command for enemy-love is followed by a clause that starts with the words "so that" (v. 45). Anytime you see the words "so that," it indicates the purpose or the result of what has just been said. In this case, the result of keeping the command to love enemies is "that you may be children of your Father in heaven" (v. 45). That result then becomes a positive outcome that substantiates the command for enemy-love. Jesus fills in the picture by describing the character of God the Father in relationship to the wicked. What is God like? He's the sort that makes the sun to rise indiscriminately on both the good and the evil. He sends rain to both the righteous and the unrighteous. These claims about God would have been particularly significant in the agrarian society of first-century Israel. Without sunshine and appropriate rainfall, the community's crops wouldn't provide a sufficient harvest to sustain its members. The point of this passage is that God treats people who oppose him with kindness. And if that's what God the Father is like, then his children should embody that aspect of his character. The children of God should love their enemies too.

Jesus makes the point again by reminding us that even tax collectors and Gentiles show love and kindness to those who love them and are kind to them. Tax collectors were often Jewish people who worked for the Roman Empire to tax the Jewish people. They were seen as compromisers with an oppressive enemy, and they often extorted money from their Jewish kinsmen. Gentiles were generally disfavored by Jewish people in the first century.

So when Jesus says that loving your neighbor and hating your enemy makes you no better than a tax collector or a Gentile, the negative force of that claim would have been exceedingly clear to his original hearers. It's not a compliment. The people of God are supposed to be better. Their character should distinguish them from everyone else. It's within this context that Jesus gives the command to be perfect.

The crucial thing is to see the parallel structure of Matthew 5:44–45 and 5:48. Look at it this way:

Verses 44–45: *Love your enemies* . . . so that you may be *children of your Father in heaven*.

Verse 48: *Be perfect*, therefore, as your *heavenly Father* is perfect.

Both of these verses call for a certain posture of the heart and then compare that posture to the character of God. The assumption is that the children should share the character of the Father and that the Father's character should be reproduced in his children. What sort of character does the Father have? He loves his enemies. What sort of character should God's children have? They should love their enemies. It is this aspect of God's character that Jesus means when he speaks of the heavenly Father's perfection. He's not talking about God's perfect knowledge or perfect power or perfect glory. He's not talking about God's eternity or omnipresence. He's talking about perfect love. God's love is perfect. And you can see that by the way he treats his enemies. He doesn't treat them badly just because they are wicked or unrighteous or because they've stood against him. He graciously gives them sun and rain and sustains their lives. His love is not conditional on their righteousness. That makes his love perfect. So when Jesus commands his hearers to *be perfect*, that's what he means. He commands a love that isn't conditional on what the other person can do for us. He calls for a love that takes the enemy as its object. If we love only those who love us, our love is conditional on what they offer us. If we love those who do not love us in return, our love is perfect. When Jesus commands his followers to *be perfect*, he means *love your enemies*. That doesn't exclude love for non-enemies. The point is that a person who is committed to loving her enemies is marked by a love that abounds to all people without regard to their attitudes or behaviors. The perfection for which he calls is perfect love. Not only is it possible, but it should be the normal character of the children of God.

This resonates deeply with what we've already seen about holiness in the Old Testament. The holiness code of Leviticus 19 reveals the character of God, who cares for people who are vulnerable and disadvantaged. Why? Because that's how God treats them. Isaiah was called to preach to people who would reject his message. He was willing to do it because he was unconditionally and unreservedly surrendered to God. He would go and love a people who would oppose him. The character Jesus calls for in the Sermon on the Mount, a character marked by perfect love, is the same character the Old Testament calls for with the language of holiness. That's why, so often, when we talk about holiness, we talk about it in terms of perfect love. Holiness isn't about a rigorous keeping of the rules for the sake of keeping the rules. Holiness is self-giving love for others—epitomized in love for enemies—for God's own sake, because he has rescued us, because he's made us his representatives, and because we love him. Will holy people obey God? Of course, if their desires are oriented to God, they will desire to obey him. But the motivation isn't some sort of legalistic self-righteousness. The motivation is a heart overflowing in love for God and neighbor. This is what it means to be holy. It means having a heart filled with perfect love.

Keeping the Law

Jesus develops his teaching on perfect love in Matthew 22:34–40. We are told that a Pharisee approached Jesus and asked him which of the commandments of God is the greatest. Jesus replied by citing Deuteronomy 6:5: "You shall love the Lord your God with all your heart, and with all your soul, and with all your mind" (Matt. 22:37). "This," Jesus said, "is the greatest and first commandment." He then went on to add a second great command: "love your neighbor as yourself" (vv. 38–39). For Jesus, these two commands sum up all the commands of the Old Testament.

It's worth noting that Jesus's teaching on perfect love in Matthew 5:48 came in the context of his teaching the true meaning of the Old Testament. Now he's asked to single out the most important Old Testament law, and he points to one that calls for perfect love. Now you may point out that the specific word *perfect* doesn't appear in these verses. And you would be right. But the idea is there. Look at it again. The command is to *love God*, and to love him in some very specific ways. Love him with *all* your heart, *all* your soul, and *all* your might. Jesus doesn't say to love God sometimes or to love God with only part of your heart, mind, or strength. No, he wants love for God that is full, whole, and complete. The command to love God with our whole heart is a call for perfect love. For Jesus, this has always been what God's self-revelation is about. From the opening pages of the Old Testament all the way through to the end, God is revealing his holy character of perfect love and seeking to form a people who embody that perfect love. When Jesus shows up, he reiterates that this is what the Old Testament was always about and calls his followers to embody a life of perfect love.

It's interesting that Jesus added the second great commandment. The Pharisee didn't ask about that. I suppose Jesus was in the mood to offer some bonus content. The crucial thing for us is that holiness (or perfect love) is not exclusively a matter of our love for God. Rather, it's a matter of love for God *and* love for our neighbors. Think about it this way. If we love God with our whole heart, mind, and strength, then that love will overflow from our lives into the lives of those around us. If we love God, we'll also love our neighbor (and our enemy!). Again, this shouldn't surprise us. After all, so much of what the Old Testament says about holiness is set in the context of how a person relates to the people around them, especially vulnerable people around them.

What Will My Life Look Like?

All this should lead us to ask, If I'm going to embody the perfect love of God, what will my life look like? The answer is that I should cultivate practices that embody love for God and practices that embody love for others. In the past, the church has called these practices *works of piety* and *works of mercy*. *Piety* is a word that describes our relationship of worship with God. *Mercy* here describes our relationship with others. Works of piety embody love for God. Works of mercy embody love for others. So when you think of works that embody love for God, think of worship and all the acts of worship in which followers of Jesus engage. We're talking about things like gathering with the church to worship God, personal prayer and devotion, and the reading of Scripture. When you think of works that embody love for others, think of ministries that care for the poor or less fortunate or the vulnerable. Sometimes this takes the form of financial gifts. Other times it involves taking our bodies out to love and serve people in relation to their needs. As we do these kinds of works, two things happen. One, we show with our bodies our love for God and neighbor. Two, our love for God and our neighbors is formed and grows. And as that happens, we become more like Jesus. His perfect love comes to fill us to overflowing. God is glorified, we are transformed, and others experience God's goodness through us. It makes sense that Jesus called love for God and love for our neighbors the most important commands.

Holiness and Perfect Love

As we reflect on what we've learned to this point, it should be increasingly clear that a character marked by holiness is the same as a character marked by perfect love. The terms should be thought of as interchangeable ways to describe the work God desires to do in his people. Both terms involve the reproduction of God's character in us. As we'll see later, this is the specific work of God's Spirit dwelling in us. The notion of holiness as perfect love also helps us avoid harmful legalistic understandings of holiness that can be quite common. Sometimes people use the language of holiness as a way of putting the burden of their behavioral standards on others. But that's not the way Scripture talks about holiness. Scripture gives us a beautiful picture of holiness as a heart filled with love for God and others. Scripture gives us a vision of holiness that looks like perfect love. Don't you want to experience perfect love?

Questions for Reflection and Discussion

1. Think of a time when someone treated you poorly. How did you respond?

2. Why should we understand the command to *be perfect* in terms of perfect love?

3. What is your response to the idea that you should love those who don't love you? Are you hesitant or resistant to the idea? Why or why not?

4. How do works of piety and works of mercy cultivate a character of perfect love for God and our neighbors? Which of these works do you practice? Which do you need begin cultivating?

5. Given what you've learned about perfect love, what does it mean to be holy? How holy can we realistically expect to be in this life? What is the relationship between grace and holiness?

6
Free to Be Fully Human

Romans

> *What then are we to say? Should we continue in sin in order that grace may abound? By no means! How can we who died to sin go on living in it? Do you not know that all of us who have been baptized into Christ Jesus were baptized into his death? Therefore we have been buried with him by baptism into death, so that, just as Christ was raised from the dead by the glory of the Father, so we too might walk in newness of life.*
>
> —Romans 6:1–4

The question of holiness drives Paul's letter to the Romans. The way he puts the question (and answers it!) in Romans 6:1–2 is especially striking. For one, the question is framed negatively in these verses: "Should we continue in sin?" Now you may be thinking, *What choice do we have? We're only human. Don't all humans sin? Isn't that what it means to be human?* And if those are the kinds of questions coming to mind, then Paul's answer to the question of sin and holiness will surprise you. Because his answer is an emphatic *no*. When Paul writes "By no means!" in verse 2, imagine him writing in all caps with multiple exclamation points. That will give you an idea of his tone and emphasis. For Paul, believers should not continue in sin. So he offers a vision of a human life that isn't characterized by sin. It's a vision of human life—*real human life!*—free from the power of sin. And while it may be surprising, it's unmistakably clear that, for Paul, sin is not essential to human life. To the contrary, sin degrades human life. Sin dehumanizes creatures made in the image of God. And normal human life—human life as God intended—is life free from sin. And if Paul is right about that, then holiness is about becoming more fully human, not less. But to grapple with that reality, we'll have to back up to the opening chapters of Romans and work our way forward.

Sin Is Against God

Paul sets out his agenda in Romans 1:16–17. He's not been to Rome, and he hasn't gotten to know the believers there. He's eager to meet them, and he wants to get them involved in his mission. But he hasn't been able to get there yet. So he writes a letter, and this letter articulates what his gospel is all about. And he's not ashamed of this gospel, because it's God's power to save all people, whether Jew or Gentile. But that raises a question. In fact, it raises two questions: What does it mean to be saved? And what do we need to be saved from? Paul starts answering the second question right away.

For Paul, human beings need to be saved from God's wrath (Romans 1:18). Now we need to be careful here, because it's easy to let our imaginations run away with the idea of God's wrath. When we hear that kind of language, we often imagine the meanest and cruelest person we can, and then we magnify all that meanness and cruelty to infinite proportions. But that's not what Paul means by "the wrath of God." No, Paul is referring to God's wise, appropriate, measured, righteous opposition to anything that seeks to destroy his good creation and anything that seeks to thwart his purposes for his good creation. God's wrath is an expression of his righteousness. If God didn't oppose sin, he wouldn't be righteous. God's wrath is his opposition to the destructive power of sin and rebellion. That's what Paul says in Romans 1:18. God's wrath is revealed against human wickedness and unrighteousness.

That raises another question: Where did that human wickedness and unrighteousness come from? And Paul's answer is quite straightforward. It came from worshipping false gods; it's the result of our idolatry. God's handiwork in creation reveals the reality of God's power and divine nature (Rom. 1:20), and human beings took the glory that belongs only to the all-wise Creator and gave it to created things—images of mortal human beings and images of various animals (1:22–23). Paul takes this to be an act of willful opposition to the truth. It's an act of rebellion. It's sin. Taken this way, sin is a willful violation of a known law. Though humans knew God, they didn't acknowledge him as God. And this teaches us something about sin. Sin is *against God.* Just as Adam rebelled against God in the garden, so all human beings—in some way or form—have rebelled *against God.* All of us have, at some point, resisted the good and wise rule of the triune God in our lives. We have insisted on our own way. We've given the honor that belongs only to our Creator to created things. When we think or act *against God*, we sin. The good news is that, despite our sin, God is committed to rescuing us. Before we get to how he rescues us, there's one more thing we need to know about sin.

Sin Is Against Nature

As the argument of Romans 1 unfolds, we learn a lot more, not only about how God responds to sin, but also about the nature of sin. We'll start with how God responds to sin.

Romans 1:24 explains that God responds to human rebellion by giving us exactly what we ask for: "Therefore God gave them up in the lusts of their hearts to impurity, to the dishonoring of their bodies among themselves" (ESV). It's as if God has said this: "If you want to live your life against me, then I'll allow you to experience the very thing you desire." And the consequences of that are significant. They include darkened hearts, darkened minds, and broken relationships with other people (especially in relation to our sexuality). We became consumed with our passions rather than God's passions (v. 26). Ultimately, our rebellion against God led to "every kind of wickedness, evil, greed and depravity" (v. 29 NIV). Paul goes so far as to say that the behaviors that arose out of depraved human desires "are contrary to nature" (v. 26 ESV). Now this is important, because it will reframe the way we think about sin and holiness. Sin, according to Paul, is unnatural. It's contrary to nature. Remember the language of degraded bodies in Romans 1:24? Our bodies are part of our human nature. When we give ourselves to sin, we don't reveal our human nature, but we degrade it. We might put it this way: sin is not only *against God*, it's also *against nature*.[3] To put

---

3. See Thomas H. McCall, *Against God and Nature: The Doctrine of Sin*, Foundations of Evangelical Theology (Wheaton: Crossway, 2019).

it a little differently, sin is unnatural. That's what we learn in Romans 1.

We've been conditioned to think of human beings as naturally sinful. Sometimes you even hear the language of human beings having a "sinful nature." But Romans 1 pushes back against that way of putting things. Human beings don't so much have a sinful nature as we have a human nature that is corrupted by sin. That's a nuanced distinction, but it's a distinction with significant implications. God created human beings to embody his character and be his representatives. As human beings, we are made in the image of God. We need to see sin as that which strips away our human nature. Sin undermines our humanity—degrades it. Human beings were created to be holy. Sin is contrary to nature. It makes us less than human. God's design for human life is holiness. Sin destroys that.

This might be a challenging concept to embrace, especially if you've been immersed in the language of "sinful nature." But consider this. There is one human being who has never sinned. His name is Jesus. He has always embodied the character of God. He has always lived in a way that pleases God the Father. He has always been holy. And he is fully and completely human, just like you and just like me. If Jesus is fully human, and if Jesus has never sinned, then human nature is not inherently sinful. It can't be. Jesus defines what it means to be fully human. And

Jesus has come to restore our full humanness by destroying the corrupting power of sin in our lives. That means salvation isn't about getting free from our sinful human nature. Salvation is about freeing our human nature from the power of sin. As that happens, we grow in holiness. And that means holiness is about becoming fully human.

Forgiveness Is Not Enough

If Jesus came to set us free from the daily power of sin in our lives, that means we need to think about salvation as something that's not limited to our experience of forgiveness and conversion. While it's absolutely true that we *need* forgiveness and we *need* conversion, it's also true that we need more than forgiveness and conversion. Paul's reasoning in Romans confirms this need. Having articulated the problem of sin in chapter 1, Paul goes on to explain how the problem will be solved. Step one is forgiveness of sin and reconciliation with God. That gets introduced beginning in Romans 3:21. Everyone has sinned (3:23). Everyone stands justly condemned. Everyone needs grace. God gives that grace through Jesus, who offered himself for our redemption. Paul explains that the shedding of Jesus's blood accomplishes our reconciliation with God. If you want to understand what's going on here, it's important to recognize that Paul earlier acknowledges the reality of God's wrath against human sin (Rom. 1:18). Because of what Jesus has done in his death and resurrection, Paul will soon say that "we have peace with God" (5:1). We move from wrath from God to peace with God. Jesus accomplishes that for us. Paul sums up this movement in Romans 3:24: "they are now justified by his grace as a gift." Justification is a legal term. It comes from the world of the Hebrew court, which looks a lot different from modern-day courts. There were no attorneys, no bailiffs, and no juries. There was a judge, an accuser, and the accused. Both were given opportunity to make their case before the judge and call witnesses to testify on their behalf. Once each case has been made, the judge would decide who was in the right. He would look on that person and declare that he or she is "justified." To be justified means the court has found a verdict in your favor. To be justified by God means that God has forgiven your sin and has accepted you into a new reconciled relationship with him. This is a gift. There's nothing we can do to earn or merit this expression of God's kindness to us. When this happens, we are saved from the penalty of our sin. We are no longer condemned. Now for a lot of people, that's basically what we mean when we talk about salvation. Perhaps you've heard someone say, "I was saved." They are probably talking about this initial experience of repentance and forgiveness. But, as we'll see, Paul is just getting warmed up. He's got a lot more to say about how the death and resurrection of Jesus save us. Paul understands that forgiveness and freedom from the penalty of sin is not enough. We need to be saved from the daily power of sin too. Paul explains this in terms of the believer's union with Christ and walking in the Spirit.

Union with Christ

Romans 6 begins with the question of holiness, even if the question is put in negative terms: "Should we continue in sin in order that grace may abound?" (v. 1). The question is repeated with slightly different wording in 6:15, "Should we sin because we are not under law but under grace?" We previously noted how some people might respond to such questions by thinking, *What choice do we have but to sin?* And if that's the way you find yourself responding, then, as we noted earlier, Paul's answer will surprise you. Paul repeatedly answers the question of whether believers should continue in sin with a resounding no! Most translations render it something like, "By no means!" Again, the thing to recognize is that Paul is very, very emphatic. This isn't a passing comment. It's not an insignificant detail. It's a crucially important point for Paul that believers are not intended to continue struggling with and succumbing to sin. How can this be? Paul points to our baptism as a marker of our union with Christ in his death. Union with

Christ means that we've been joined so closely to Jesus that everything that is true of him is also true of us. Paul reasons this way: if we've been brought into union with the crucified Messiah, then we are dead to sin. And if the Messiah has been raised to new life, then we can walk in *newness of life* (v. 4) that anticipates our future participation in Christ's bodily resurrection (v. 5). That newness of life is a life lived free from the power of sin.

Paul goes on to say that union with Christ means that we've died with Christ. It also means that we will be raised bodily from the dead, just as Christ was. What does it mean to have died with Christ? To understand what Paul means, you need to understand two terms: "old self" and "body of sin" (v. 6). By *old self*, Paul means the self under slavery to sin and estranged from God. This is our reality prior to forgiveness and justification. *Body of sin* means the physical body under the power of sin. This power, Paul insists, is destroyed through union with Christ. To be clear, our bodies are not destroyed, but sin's power in our bodies is destroyed through union with Christ. That means that our bodies are free from slavery to sin and enabled to be holy. Jesus has died and was raised. Believers have been deeply connected with him in his death such that we will one day share in his resurrection. That means that we must now behave as if we are dead to sin (because we are!) and live as the kind of people God will raise bodily from the dead.

People who've died to sin and are awaiting their resurrection should be the sort of people who honor and please God with their lives. Another word for that sort of life is *holy*. Sometimes we see holiness as a negative idea that means we don't get to have any fun. But that's not how Paul sees it. Paul offers hope by declaring that freedom from sin and the subsequent process of sanctification (or increasing holiness) is for our advantage (v. 22). Did you hear that? God's work to make us holy is given for our advantage. It means we don't have to live as slaves to all the thoughts and behaviors that leave us feeling guilty and ashamed and condemned. God gives the advantage of holiness, and he gives it through union with Christ.

Walking in the Spirit

If Romans 6 explains how Christ is at work in our sanctification, Romans 8 explains how the Spirit contributes to it too. Paul sets this up in terms of a big contrast between "the flesh" and "the Spirit." Now you need to understand that when Paul talks about the flesh in Romans 8, he's not talking about your skin or any part of your body. For Paul, the flesh is a way of talking about two things. First, the flesh is a power that is operative on us that makes us captive to sin. We see this power at work in Romans 7:18 where Paul describes how people who are not yet justified and who do not yet have the Holy Spirit within them are unable to will what is right. This is reiterated in 7:25: "With my flesh I am a slave to the law of sin." In the flesh, we are slaves to sin. We don't have the ability to stop sinning. The flesh is a way of talking about that power that holds us captive. Second, the flesh also describes our complicity with sin. This comes through in Romans 8:4–7 where Paul talks about how people walk according to the flesh, live according to the flesh, and set their minds on the things of the flesh. Note how in each one of these the human being is the agent who is cooperating with the flesh as an active and complicit partner in sin.[4]

How then is the flesh defeated? How do we get freed from it? Paul's answer is that those who have been joined in union with Christ are also given the gift of the Holy Spirit to dwell within their bodies. People who are ruled by the flesh and who walk in the flesh are unable to please God. But Paul declares to the Christians in Rome (and to us!): "You are not in the flesh; you are in the Spirit" (8:9). The clear implication is that you *can* live in a way that pleases God. You don't have to sin. You are free to be holy. You are free to be fully human.

---

4. Cf. Susan Grove Eastman, *Paul and the Person: Reframing Paul's Anthropology* (Grand Rapids: Eerdmans, 2017), 110–11.

Are you beginning to see why a truncated gospel is so dangerous? It's because a gospel of forgiveness alone leaves us without the beautifully good news of freedom from the daily power of sin. It leaves us with the sad implication that God offers forgiveness but not freedom. It suggests that we can escape from hell, but we just have to put up with the continuing reality of our sin. Paul tells a very different story. Jesus has joined us to himself, and the Spirit has taken residence in our bodies, for the express purpose of enabling us to stop sinning and to live lives that embody love for God and neighbor. That's the rest of the gospel. And that's very good news.

Questions for Reflection and Discussion

1. What do you think about the claim that sin is not inherent or essential to human life but degrades our humanity instead? Is that a new idea? How does Romans 1 help us see this reality?

2. What does it mean to walk in the flesh? What does it mean to walk in the Spirit? Are there areas of fleshliness in your life that need to be brought in step with the Holy Spirit?

3. What are some ways you can cultivate walking in the Spirit?

4. Christians often console one another with appeals to falling *back* on the grace of God when we fail or sin. Can grace also propel us forward? If grace is limitless, can it also do the work of reorienting us away from sin and toward God?

5. What words, images, or experiences would you use to describe union with Christ? Is being made fully alive in him something you desire?

7
What Is God's Will for Me?

1 Thessalonians and Philippians

> *Finally, brothers and sisters, we ask and urge you in the Lord Jesus that, as you learned from us how you ought to live and to please God (as, in fact, you are doing), you should do so more and more. For you know what instructions we gave you through the Lord Jesus. For this is the will of God, your sanctification: that you abstain from fornication; that each one of you know how to control your own body in holiness and honor, not with lustful passion, like the Gentiles who do not know God; that no one wrong or exploit a brother or sister in this matter, because the Lord is an avenger in all these things, just as we have already told you beforehand and solemnly warned you. For God did not call us to impurity but in holiness. Therefore*

*whoever rejects this rejects not human authority
but God, who also gives his Holy Spirit to you.*
—1 Thessalonians 4:1–8

Let the same mind be in you that was in Christ Jesus.
—Philippians 2:5

What is God's will for me? I've heard that question asked by people of all ages, whether college students, middle-aged folks, or senior adults. We want to know what God wants for us and from us. Usually, the question focuses on major life decisions. *Should we make this move? Should I marry this person? Should I take this job? What is God's purpose for me in retirement?* All those questions are important, but sometimes we overcomplicate things. The apostle Paul sees it much more simply. God's will for us is focused on one thing and only one thing, namely, our holiness. That's what he says in 1 Thessalonians 4:3, "For this is the will of God, your sanctification." Sanctification is the process through which God makes us holy. For Paul, the question of God's will isn't as much about what to do next as it is about who we are becoming. The question of God's will is really the question of holiness. But what does that mean?

Not a Bonus Level

In my experience, if people think about holiness at all, they often think of it as a bonus level for spectacular Christians. Holiness isn't for everyone, they would say; and if it's for anyone, it's for very advanced and mature believers who've been walking with God for a really, really long time. The most devoted folks get rewarded with the bonus level. Everyone else just has to stumble along. Sanctification is for the saints, but most of us aren't saints. The problem with that way of thinking is that Paul doesn't talk about sanctification and holiness in that way. He portrays holiness as a starting point for all believers, not a special reward for a few. God's will for every believer is growth in holiness. God's will for you and me is that we embody his character and that we do so more and more.

Paul thinks of holiness in terms of a life that is pleasing to God. Note that he says the Thessalonians are already living to please God, and he exhorts them to "do so more and more" (v. 1). Paul doesn't portray them as people who've reached the finish line or any kind of bonus level. The whole point of a finish line is that you don't have to run any more. If you get to a bonus level, then you've already completed the main task. You're done. For Paul, holiness isn't about finishing something;

holiness is the starting point and ongoing posture of our daily living. The life pleasing to God isn't out of reach; it should be the *normal* Christian life. Paul's language of "more and more" highlights that point. A life pleasing to God isn't a matter of some future achievement but is, instead, a continuing posture of growth in the present. We mistakenly think of holiness as something we might get to later. Paul thinks of holiness as the present fruit of walking with Jesus. Holiness isn't something we have to get to so we can be done. Holiness is a constant practice of surrender to God now.

It may help to think about cultivating a healthy lifestyle. If we want to be physically healthy, we have to always attend to it. We have to do certain things like exercise and eat the right foods. And when we become healthy, we don't stop paying attention to our health. We never get to the point where we're healthy enough to quit focusing on our health. We never finish. Good health is more a lifestyle, not a singular goal. The healthiest people in the world are the ones who are always working on their health. They do so more and more.

Holiness is like that. The people who consistently embody God's character don't treat holiness as a goal to reach or a status to obtain. It's the normal and continuing practice of offering oneself to God in love. It's also worth remembering that the church in Thessalonica is relatively young with fairly recent converts. Paul may have written this letter only weeks or months after his first visit. These folks haven't been at it for long. The Thessalonians are normal Christian disciples, just like you and me, and Paul wants them to see that God's will for them *now* is holiness.

Not a Special Few

If we're tempted to think that holiness is only for a few really special Christians, it's important to recognize that Paul commands all the Thessalonians to cultivate holiness as a normal orientation of their lives. This, he says, is God's calling to us—*all of us* (v. 7). The call to a consistently holy life is for every believer. Paul doesn't suggest that the life pleasing to God is just for the clergy or experienced disciples. This letter is addressed to the whole church in Thessalonica (v. 1). God calls all his people to a life of holiness. Paul even goes so far as to say that rejecting this is a rejection of God's own authority (v. 8). This shouldn't surprise us, of course. It resonates deeply with everything we've learned so far, whether in the Old Testament or the New Testament. Paul also reminds the recipients that God is the one who gives his own Holy Spirit to dwell in them. While Paul doesn't go into detail here about the role of the Holy Spirit in graciously producing a life of holiness in God's people, his mention of the Spirit nevertheless resonates with the reality that anyone who has the Spirit also has everything necessary to consistently embody the character of God. If you have the Spirit, you have what you need.

What Does It Look Like?

So what does it look like for normal people to consistently live to please God? Paul connects it with the control of our bodies (and that's why I often speak of holiness as *embodying* God's character). In particular, he mentions the control of the body with regard to sexuality. The New Revised Standard Version uses the word *fornication* (v. 3), but the word in Paul's Greek is *porneia* and refers to all sexual sin. In the ancient world, it was common for men to engage in exploitative and competitive sexual behaviors, and they held most of the social power. Unmarried women, in particular, were quite vulnerable to the sexual advances of men in their society. In that setting, Paul frames holiness as a matter of self-control in contrast to indulging in one's lust. That first-century reality has application beyond its original context. Indeed, many people are wrestling with what it means to be holy and aren't involved in exploitative relationships. Here's the principle that emerges out of Paul's comments to the Thessalonians: holiness means self-denial and concern for the other. It means not looking at other people as objects of our own self-satisfaction. It means looking at others with a heart of overflowing love. This, for Paul, marks out the difference between believers and unbelievers. Believers honor God by seeking what's best for others rather than looking for ways to use them.

It's All a Gift

Throughout this book, we've been reflecting on two questions. What is holiness? How holy can we reasonably expect to become? So far in this chapter we've been focused on the first one. Holiness is God's will for his people to live to please him by embodying self-control and love for others. But what about the second question? How holy can we really be? Paul speaks to this question in 1 Thessalonians 5:23: "May the God of peace himself sanctify you entirely." Many have wondered whether those of us in the Wesleyan tradition are justified in using the language of *entire sanctification*. I believe we are justified, and I believe it because that very language appears here in the Bible. For Paul, the scope of sanctification is our whole selves. God wants to transform every part of us and leave nothing about us unchanged. According to Paul, God can do this *entirely*. The point is reiterated when he mentions God keeping the believer's "spirit and soul and body" sound and blameless. Paul isn't saying that human beings are composed of three parts with one part called *spirit*, another part called *soul*, and a third part called *body*. No, this is Paul's way of saying that our whole selves—every part of us!—can be kept by God in holiness. Nothing is left out. The whole scope of our being can be made whole.

What's even more striking is that God is the one who does the work. God doesn't tell the recipients to sanctify themselves. He tells them that God is able to sanctify them entirely. God is the one who does it. It's a work of his grace. It's a gift. Sometimes people talk like we get converted and justified by grace, but then we have to work to get our sanctification. Paul would reject that way of speaking. Sanctification is a part of God's saving work, and all salvation is offered as a gift of grace received by faith. God gives the gift of holiness. We trust him to do it, and we embody that trust by continuously offering ourselves to him. Maybe it seems too good to be true. Maybe that's why Paul reiterates his point in 5:24, that God "is faithful, and he will do this."

And he wants to do it now. Notice that Paul sets the sanctifying work of God in relation to the second coming of Jesus. He doesn't say that believers will become sound and blameless (that is, entirely sanctified) after Jesus returns. No, Paul says that God will keep you sound and blameless between now and the time Jesus returns. That, my friends, is good news. It means that the power of sin in our daily lives doesn't have to be the power that rules our daily lives. It means that we can be free from blameworthy things. It means that God is able to make us holy, and he's able to do it now, and he's able to keep us in holiness to the day when Jesus returns. That's the rest of the gospel. It's the part we often forget.

The Mind of Christ

There's one more place to go before we leave the letters of Paul. The language of holiness doesn't figure prominently in Philippians, but the concept of Christlikeness does. Philippians also contains a verse in which Paul is happy to use the language of perfection regarding his own life. That one is shocking to many. Let's start with Christlikeness; then we'll see if we can sort out Paul's language of perfection.

In Philippians 2:5, Paul instructs, "Let the same mind be in you that was in Christ Jesus." This command runs parallel to a couple of other commands he's already given just a few verses before. To understand this one, we need to start with those. What are they? The first one is "do nothing from selfish ambition or conceit, but in humility regard others as better than yourselves" (v. 3). The second is "let each of you look not to your own interests, but to the interests of others" (v. 4). You need to know that there was some budding factionalism in Philippi, and that Paul was writing to cultivate concord among the recipients. He needs them to remain unified. Otherwise, it'll be hard for the gospel to go forward in their city. The conflict seems related to a disagreement between two women leaders in the church. Paul calls them by name in Philippians 4:2 and urges them to work out their differences. The commands in 2:3–4 pave the way for the coming call for unity. They've got to put away ambition and any self-oriented vying for position. They've got to consider the interests of others ahead of their own. In other words, set your interests to the side and focus on what's best for others. Paul says this is done "in humility" (v. 3). Now you need to know that while humility is a virtue in our day, but this was not the case in the ancient world. No self-respecting Roman citizen of Philippi would ever think of himself as humble. Slaves were humble. The poor were humble. Romans were not humble. Paul's original readers were more likely to see humility as a vice than a virtue. But Paul calls for humility regardless. He wants to see them embody other-oriented concern and love. And then he connects that posture to Jesus. Let the posture that Jesus took also characterize your life. Have the mind of Christ.

Paul fleshes out what he means by describing the self-giving and self-lowering love of Jesus. Paul recognized the divinity of Jesus. That's what he means when he says that Jesus is "in the form of God" (v. 6). And it's *because* Jesus is God that he doesn't exploit his privileged position, but instead lowers himself and dies the death of a slave on a cross. Jesus didn't seek his own interests. Jesus wasn't motivated by selfish ambition. Jesus looked to our interests—yours and mine—rather than his own. And we know this, because anyone who goes willingly to a cross for the sake of another is not going because he's seeking his own interests. No, he's seeking your best interests and mine. That sort of self-giving love is the mind of Christ, and that posture resonates with what we've learned about holiness to this point. Holiness is Christlikeness, and Christlikeness is other-oriented love.

Did Paul Think He Was Perfect?

Paul does something funny with the language of perfection in Philippians 3:12 and 3:15. In verse 12, he says that he has not been made perfect. In verse 15, he puts himself in a group called "those of us who are perfect." Different translations render both verses in different ways to try to deal with the problem, but Paul uses the same Greek root word in both instances. It's the same root word Jesus used when he said, "Be perfect," in Matthew 5:48. So, what's going on? What does Paul mean?

To start with, Paul does not contradict himself. When he says that he's not perfect in verse 12 and that he is perfect in verse 15, he's using the same root word in two different ways. Paul does this on occasion. Consider Romans 9:6, "not all who are descended from Israel are Israel" (NIV). He's clearly using the language of "Israel" in two different ways. To understand what Paul means in Philippians 3, the context is crucial. In verse 12, he's just finished describing his hope to be raised from the dead when Jesus returns. And it's that final perfection of the resurrected body that he doesn't yet have. In verse 15, the most important clue comes in the way he phrases the command: the perfect are those who have the *same mind*. That one word—*mind*—recalls everything he said about the mind of Christ in chapter 2. When Paul describes himself and others as "those who are perfect," he means those who have the mind of Christ. Just as in Matthew 5:48, "perfect" is not referring to divine perfections that are only true of God. It doesn't mean no mistakes or no faults or no mess-ups. It means looking not to your own interests but to the interests of others. For Paul, this language of perfection means other-oriented love.

Conclusion

So, in both 1 Thessalonians and Philippians, Paul calls upon Christians to embody self-giving and other-focused love. This is what he means by holiness. This is what he means by the language of perfection. We might find his language surprising. Some might even find it troubling. But the language is what it is. The most important thing is to discover what the language means and then live into it. The good news is that our living into a life of holiness is a gift of God's grace.

Questions for Reflection and Discussion

1. Is the idea of holiness (or perfection) as other-oriented love new to you? If so, how?

2. What are some areas in your life that are marked by self-interest? What would it look like for the Holy Spirit to transform those areas of life? Are you willing to surrender to that work of the Spirit of God?

3. Scripture says that God is the one who makes us holy. Have you ever pursued holiness in your own strength? If so, what was the outcome? What needs to change?

4. Have you ever been a part of a group of three to five same-gendered people who meet together regularly to become the love of God for one another and the world? What would being part of such a group, where you are fully known and fully loved, affect the trajectory of your life? Learn more at discipleshipbands.com.

5. Is holiness and a saintly identity something you are willing to embrace, or does it still seem like the call for an extraordinary few? How does Scripture challenge you or console you?

8
Why Did Jesus Come?

1 John

> *My little children, I am writing these things to you so that you may not sin.*
>
> —1 John 2:1a

> *Beloved, let us love one another, because love is from God; everyone who loves is born of God and knows God. Whoever does not love does not know God, for God is love. God's love was revealed among us in this way: God sent his only Son into the world so that we might live through him. In this is love, not that we loved God but that he loved us and sent his Son to be the atoning sacrifice for our sins. Beloved, since God loved us so much, we also ought to love one another. No one has ever seen*

> *God; if we love one another, God lives in us, and his love is perfected in us.*
>
> —1 John 4:7–12

It's shocking. Does the author of 1 John really think that his writings can enable the recipients to stop sinning? Because that's what he says. If we think of sin as inherent and essential to human life, then the words of 1 John 2:1 boggle the mind. But it says what it says. John wrote this letter as a means of grace to help his first recipients (and us!) to not sin. Maybe that should reframe the way we think about sin in relation to human life. For John, sin is not essential to human being. Jesus came to deal with sin so that we can stop sinning. John writes to share that good news with all of us.

Don't Deceive Yourself

I speak with people about holiness a lot. People sometimes respond with skepticism (and sometimes antagonism), and they often quote 1 John 1:8, "If we say that we have no sin, we deceive ourselves, and the truth is not in us." There it is, they say—everyone has sin. To think otherwise is to engage in self-deception. This is sometimes taken as obvious evidence that the view of holiness set forth in this book is plainly wrong. The trouble with that approach is that the same person who wrote 1 John 1:8 also wrote 1 John 2:1, "I am writing these things to you so that you may not sin." The two belong together and do not contradict one another. For John, we all have sin, but we don't have to sin. Everyone comes into the world in sin and with a sinful posture. If we claim otherwise, we lie to ourselves. But that damaged condition is exactly what Jesus came to restore. So John calls upon his readers to confess their sin and promises that Jesus is faithful and just and will cleanse believers of sin (1:9). He reiterates the point that anyone who thinks they've never had a sin problem is a liar and makes Jesus a liar (v. 10). But that doesn't change the fact that Jesus came to cleanse us and free us from a life lived in the darkness of sin. That's exactly why Jesus came—to deal with our sin so that it no longer characterizes our lives. John writes to share this good news so that those who hear can stop sinning. That's why Jesus came. That's why John wrote.

So for John, the normal Christian life is not a life characterized by sin, but that doesn't mean it's impossible for Christians to sin. He acknowledges this in 1 John 2:1b, "But if anyone does sin, we have an advocate with the Father, Jesus Christ the righteous." This is important, because sometimes people grab on to the language of holiness (or entire sanctification) and go on to claim that they can't sin ever again. They think it's impossible for them to sin. But Scripture doesn't talk about it that way. For as long as we're alive, it will be possible for us to sin against God. The work of Christ for us and the work of the Spirit in us make it possible for us to not sin, but they don't make it impossible for us to sin. The possibility of sin will be with us the whole of our lives, even though the reality of sin is not to characterize our lives. *If* we sin, we have Jesus, who loves us and pleads his own sacrifice in our place before his Father and ours. He is our advocate. He forgives us. He cleanses us. He enables us to live to please God. But this isn't like flipping a switch such that it's impossible to go back to a life of sin. It's quite possible, but it need not be.

Instead of going back to a life of sin, John calls us to go forward in a life of obedience to God. John uses the image of walking with God to illustrate the point. If we abide in God, then we ought to walk as he walks (2:6). God's life should be present in our lives. God's character should shape our character. That's what it means to walk with him. We can *say* we walk with him and still *live* in sin, but John says the person who does that is a liar. Walking with God means walking in obedience to God. Then John says this: "Whoever obeys his word, truly in this person the love of God has reached perfection" (2:5). Now that might surprise you, but honestly at this point in the book, it shouldn't. We've seen the language of perfect love before. We shouldn't be surprised to find it here. John, like other biblical authors, believes and writes that it is possible for God's love to be perfected in us. That's the life of obedience to God. It's a life that is pleasing to God. It's a life of holiness before God. And it's supposed to be the normal Christian life.

The Old Commandment and the New Commandment

What does it look like "to walk just as he walked" (2:6)? John fills in the picture for us in 2:7–17. He sets up two contrasting commandments—one is an old commandment (v. 7) and the other is a new commandment (v. 8). John doesn't say explicitly what the old commandment is. But obedience to God that is embodied in love for God and others is a consistent theme of the letter, and in the immediate context he condemns those who hate their brothers and sisters while commending love for brothers and sisters. It's likely, therefore, that John has in mind the "new command of Jesus" in the gospel of John 13:34: "A new commandment I give to you, that you love one another" (ESV). It was a new command when Jesus gave it; by the time 1 John was written, it's "no new commandment," but it's still "the word that you have heard" (2:7).

But what is the new commandment that John now writes to believers? We get an answer to that question by looking for the first imperative to come after John declares his intent to write a new commandment in 2:8. That imperative comes in 2:15: "Do not love the world or the things in the world." This is the new thing John writes. To summarize, I'm suggesting that the old commandment John is thinking about is the commandment of Jesus to love one another (John 13:34), and the new commandment John is writing is the exhortation not to love the world and the things of the world (1 John 2:15). You can see how the two stand alongside one another and complement one another. Love for God is obedience to Jesus embodied in love for others. This requires a resistance to loving the things of the world. John sees these as mutually exclusive. Love for God and love for the world stand in opposition to one another. We cannot offer our affections to both. What does John mean when he speaks of the things of the world? He's working in broad categories: "The desire of the flesh, the desire of the eyes, the pride in riches" (2:16). The "desire of the flesh" likely involves self-oriented sexual lusts. The "desire of the eyes" evokes the notion of coveting things that are not ours. And "pride in riches" clearly addresses the human attempt to build up oneself with wealth that attempts to satisfy the longings of our hearts. Lust, greed, and pride—what's the common theme here? All involve desires and affections governed by self-interest. Like Paul in the letter to the Philippians, John recognizes that self-interest is antithetical to love for God. Love for the world and the things of the world reveal a human heart curved in on itself, not a human heart offered to God and neighbor. Don't love the things of the world. Love the people God has placed around you.

The Question of Perfect Love

All that may seem quite straightforward. Of course, God wants us to love others. Do we really need a whole study to teach us that? Well, John isn't quite finished. He also wants us to discover the beautiful reality that love for God and neighbor can be perfected in us. That's the language he uses in 1 John 4:12. In just a moment, John will declare that "God is love" (4:16). This is the only conclusion that can be reached when we consider that "God sent his only Son into the world so that we might live through him" (4:9). John sees the sending of Jesus as an expression of the eternal perfect love that God the Father, Son, and Spirit have for one another.

It's worth taking a moment to consider the claim that God is love. There are many ways to describe God: God is the creator; God is sovereign; God is the judge; God is the savior. But all those claims describe God in relation to us.

God created us. God is sovereign over us. God is the judge of us. God is our savior. What if we wanted to describe God, not with reference to us, but with reference to himself? How would we do that? What word describes God apart from anything temporal or anything he has made? The word is *love*. Consider this. Before God made anything, for eternity, the Father loved the Son and the Spirit; the Son loved the Father and the Spirit; the Spirit loved the Father and the Son. God is love because God is the Trinity—one God in three persons, three persons who exist in eternal relationships of perfect love. God's purpose for you and me is to make us participants in that perfect love, and we don't have to wait for it. He wants to do it now, and the Bible says he can do it now.

This is why Jesus came. He came to incorporate us into the perfect love of Father, Son, and Spirit. That love comes to perfection in us when we honor God with our lives by loving the people around us and remaining undistracted by the things of the world. Yes, Jesus came to forgive our sins, but he came for so much more than that. He came to fill us with his perfect love. Remember that this is not about striving to obey a list of rules for the sake of the rules. This is about experiencing the love of God so fully that it fills us and overflows into the people around us. Yes, it requires self-denial, but it's not a life of grueling struggle under sin.

It's a life that resists sin in order to embody the richness of the beauty of the perfect love of God—Father, Son, and Spirit. Let me say again, this is why Jesus came: to bring the love of God to perfection in us.

You may have already noticed the missional implications of this. Walking with Jesus—worshipping him—bears fruit in holiness embodied in love for others. If we draw near to him, our lives will be aimed at our neighbors and the nations, and our hearts will be driven to draw others into the same experience of his perfect love that has filled us to overflowing. Devotion to Jesus results in holiness that overflows in other-oriented missional love.

Back to the Question

Now you might be thinking that we haven't talked much about holiness in this chapter. Remember that concepts related to holiness can be present even when the specific word *holiness* is not. That's what we have in 1 John. It should be clear that John's language of perfect love is getting at the same concept that holiness language describes elsewhere in Scripture. Holiness is an experience of God's perfect love that shows forth in us in love for others, whether friend or enemy. Holiness, sanctification, perfect love—all of these terms get at the same central reality.

Take a moment to envision the sort of life we're talking about. It's a life marked by love for God. That sort of life is one in which we offer ourselves to God in love with a view toward being rid of sin and growing in virtue. Love for God means cultivating humility and not seeking honor from other people. This comes to characterize our lives more and more as we engage in practices that embody love for God—reading Scripture, private prayer and devotion, gathering with the church to worship, and participating in the sacraments. These practices cultivate in us a growing love for God and an appropriate view of our own insufficiency apart from God's grace. Along the way, we grow in love for God. We develop an increasing sense of peace and the assurance of his love. We grow in gentleness. We discover deepening joy as we walk more and more closely with God.

We began this study with two questions related to holiness. What is holiness? How holy can we expect to be in this life? From the perspective of 1 John, holiness means that God's love is poured in us to such an extent that sin is pushed out. Our love for the things of the world is replaced by love for God in Christ and the Spirit. How wide is this work of God? John describes this as love being perfected in us. The scope of God's work is complete and full. No aspect of our being is left out.

Questions for Reflection and Discussion

1. What's the difference between what John calls the "old commandment" and the "new commandment"? How do they relate to each other? How are they embodied in your life?

2. Are there areas of your life that are attracted to the things of the world? What practices do you employ to resist loving the things of the world?

3. What does the Bible mean by holiness? What evidence do you see in your life that God is making you holy?

4. Do you believe the promise of Scripture that God can sanctify you entirely? Do you want God to sanctify you entirely?

5. What must change in your life for you to become entirely sanctified?

CONCLUSION

What is holiness? How holy can we expect to become in this life? Those two questions have been the focus of this study. Let's take a moment to summarize our key discoveries in relation to those questions.

The Language of Holiness

To start, let's review our principle that the word *holiness* doesn't have to be present for a text to shape our understanding of holiness. It's common in biblical interpretation to recognize that concepts can be present even when this or that specific word is not. And holiness is about God's people living into his purpose for them. As a result, we've looked at a variety of biblical terms to shape our understanding of God's transforming work to actualize his purposes in his people—sanctification, perfection, holiness. These terms have been used somewhat interchangeably in this study, because Scripture uses all of them to get at the reality that God's purpose for us is that we come to share his character in order that we may faithfully represent him to others. Look for the concept, not just the word.

Embodying God's Character

What does it mean to be holy? It means the people of God embody the character of God. Again and again, God reminds his people that he is holy and that they, too, must be holy. God doesn't mean they have to be like him in terms of his unshared attributes. God is eternal, all-knowing, and present everywhere. We will never be those things. God means his people must be like him in terms of his character. God always does what he ought to do. Therefore, the people of God must always do likewise. This is rooted in the reality that we represent God to our neighbors and the nations, and our lives always tell some story about our God. The story we tell with our lives will either be true or false. When believers sin, our lives tell a lie about God. When we honor him with our lives, our character testifies truly about his character. Holiness means telling the truth about God's character with the character of our lives.

Perfect Love

If we want to know what holiness is, we have to talk about perfect love. Yes, the language of *perfection* can be surprising or even off-putting. Nevertheless, Scripture repeatedly uses that language to describe God's purpose for his people, not because God is a perfectionist, but because his love is perfect. So, Jesus commands his followers to be perfect as the heavenly Father is perfect (Matt. 5:48). But he doesn't mean that in an unqualified sense. He carefully articulated this perfection in terms of love for enemies. If you want to be like God, love your enemies. Enemy-love is perfect love. Now you might be thinking, *I don't really have any enemies*. The point is that enemy-love is the most extensive sort of love. That's why the Bible associates it with perfect love. Perfect love includes love for acquaintances and friends, but it goes beyond that. Perfect love is offered even to those who don't return love to us. It holds nothing back and comes with no conditions.

Paul and John likewise link perfection and love. In Philippians, Paul calls on believers to put the interests of others ahead of their own (2:3–4) and highlights this aspect of Jesus's own character revealed in his incarnation and death (2:5–11). Then, again perhaps surprisingly, Paul attaches the language of perfection to the posture of other-oriented love in believers. He even uses the language of perfection to describe himself and others (Phil. 3:15 NASB). The common theme is that the people of God are to embody the character of God. God's character is revealed in Jesus, and it is revealed to be marked by self-giving love. Thus, God's people should embody the character of God embodied by Jesus—self-sacrificial and other-oriented love. We also saw that 1 John doesn't shy away from the language of perfection either. John says straightforwardly that the antidote to sin is a life of obedient love to God, and this love can be brought to perfection in us (4:12, 17). What does perfect love look like for John? It looks like love for God and love for others (4:20–21). The language of *perfection* may be unsettling, but it is manifestly biblical language. If we're willing to deal with that, we may find that a deep experience of God's kindness comes with it.

Holiness Is Normal

Another recurring theme is that holiness should be the normal posture of the Christian life. We are often taught that sin is essential to human life, and that a life consistently free from sin is impossible. The trouble with that is that Scripture repeatedly tells believers to stop sinning. We saw this especially in Romans 6:1, 15, and 1 John 2:1. When the question of sin arises, the writers of the Bible never say that there's nothing we can do about it because it's part of our nature. They always respond to the question of sin in the life of the believer by saying something like this: *stop it!* This is because the Bible portrays holiness as normal for the people of God. In 1 Thessalonians 4:3, holiness is the starting point for the life of Christian discipleship, not a goal for later maturity or a bonus round for really great Christians. Likewise in Romans, believers are to walk in newness of life because union with Christ means they are dead to sin (6:1–11). Let's get used to this biblical idea: *holiness* should be the word that defines the normal Christian life.

Holiness Means Fully Human

We've recognized that sin isn't essential to human nature. We can go further. Holiness is the heart of what it means to live human life to the full. Take a moment to consider God's vision for normal human life. God didn't design us to be consistently stumbling under the power of sin. He designed human life to tell the truth about his character. That means growth in holiness is growth into a more full experience of human life as God intends it. Yes, we've all sinned. But there is one human being who has never sinned. His name is Jesus, and he became fully human and remains fully human. In his person, human nature and God's nature were united. As a fully human being, he has never sinned. He has never set himself against God or nature. And if there is one fully human being who has never sinned, then sin cannot be essential to human nature. We learned in Romans 1:18–32 that sin is actually against human nature. Sin degrades human nature, tears it down, and make us less than fully human. The work of God to make us holy is the restoration of our human nature, not freedom from it. Growth in holiness means growth in Christlikeness. And if Jesus defines what it means to be human, then growth in holiness means we are becoming more like the most fully human One. Let this sink in: holiness means fully human.

Entire Sanctification

Are we justified in speaking of *entire* sanctification? Some would say that we are not, even though Scripture repeatedly speaks of holiness in terms of its comprehensive scope. Isaiah gave God his unconditional *yes*. Nothing in the prophet's heart was held back when God asked, "Who will go?" (6:8). Was he not *entirely* given to God's call? Ezekiel offered hope that God would cleanse his people of *all* their uncleanness and idolatry (36:25). Paul prayed for the Thessalonians that they would be entirely sanctified (1 Thess. 5:23). As best I can tell, Scripture consistently portrays sanctification as comprehensive in scope. There is no aspect of human nature that God is unable or uneager to touch with the power of his transforming grace. So are we justified in speaking of *entire* sanctification? The clear answer is *yes*, because the Bible itself uses that very language.

The reason Scripture uses that language is because sanctification is a work of grace. God does it, not us. Must we cooperate with God by not sinning? Yes, of course. But even that is enabled by the presence of his Holy Spirit. It's not a matter of striving to be better; it is a matter of surrendering to God's grace. Stop working against God. Paul told the Thessalonians that God would accomplish their entire sanctification (1 Thess. 5:24). Ezekiel told the Hebrew people that God would give them a new and thoroughly obedient heart (36:26). So when you feel defeated and unable to honor God with your life, remember and take refuge in the knowledge that he alone is able to keep you from falling (Jude 24–25). He is the one who sanctifies you. He will do it, and he wants to do it entirely. He won't do it against our will. He requires our cooperation and surrender to his work. Nevertheless, the power to transform us is ultimately the power of God.

Worship, Holiness, and Mission

Several texts we considered are linked to these three concepts. Holiness is always rooted and grows out of a relationship of devotion to the triune God. Worshipping God, obeying Jesus, walking in the Spirit—all of these get at the deep reality that God desires communion with those he has made to bear his image. When we worship God (and not idols) as he ought to be worshipped, we grow in likeness to him. We increasingly share his character. We become a holy people who walk with our holy God. But that's not all. The holiness of the people of God is crucial to the mission of the church. Holiness produces the mission. Holiness is the mission. I cannot escape Ezekiel 36:23: "And the nations shall know that I am the Lord, says the Lord God, when through you I display my holiness before their eyes." How will the nations know who God is and what he is like? Only when the people of God consistently embody the holiness of God. If the nations of the world are to know God, then the people of God must be like him. And as the nations perceive God's character in us, they will be drawn to him, and they will come to know him, and they will come to share his character too. The ground of holiness is worship. The goal of holiness is mission.

The Question of Holiness

What is holiness? How holy can we be? To the first question, holiness is a life turned away from self-interest and marked by love for God and your neighbor (and enemy).

Holiness doesn't mean we won't experience temptation. It doesn't mean we won't sin. It does mean we don't have to sin when tempted. Instead of choosing to chase after sin, the Holy Spirit who dwells in us can enable us to choose to chase after God. This is God's purpose for us. Sin and self-interest rob us of experiencing God's best for us. Jesus offers so much more. He offers healing, fullness, restoration, wholeness, and holiness. He offers a life of perfect love.

What about that second question? How holy can we expect to be in this life? To that question, I only remind you of the testimony of Scripture that we have heard. God has promised to cleanse his people of *all* their idols. God has declared his desire to sanctify you *entirely*. God is able to bring his love to *perfection* in you. The consistent testimony of Scripture—Old Testament and New Testament—is that God's will for you is holiness, not partial holiness, but full holiness. So, what can you expect? Expect him to do what he has promised to do. Expect him to cleanse you and to cleanse you fully. Expect him to sanctify you and to sanctify you entirely. Expect him to bring his love to perfection in your life. Don't strive for it. Surrender to it. "The one who calls you is faithful, and he will do this" (1 Thess. 5:24).

AN INVITATION TO AWAKENING

This resource comes with an invitation.

The invitation is as simple as it is comprehensive. It is not an invitation to commit your life to this or that cause or to join an organization or to purchase another book. The invitation is this: to wake up to the life you always hoped was possible and the reason you were put on planet Earth. It begins with following Jesus Christ.

In case you are unaware, Jesus was born in the first century BCE into a poor family from Nazareth, a small village located in what is modern-day Israel. While his birth was associated with extraordinary phenomena, we know little about his childhood. At approximately thirty years of age, Jesus began a public mission of preaching, teaching, and healing throughout the region known as Galilee. His mission was characterized by miraculous signs and wonders; extravagant care of the poor and marginalized; and multiple unconventional claims about his own identity and purpose. In short, he claimed to be the incarnate Son of God with the mission and power to save people from sin, deliver them from death, and bring them into the now-and-eternal kingdom of God—"on earth as it is in heaven" (Matt. 6:10).

In the spring of his thirty-third year, during the Jewish Passover celebration, Jesus was arrested by the religious authorities, put on trial in the middle of the night, and at their urging, sentenced to death by a Roman governor. On the day known to history as Good Friday, Jesus was crucified on a Roman cross and then was buried in a borrowed tomb. On the following Sunday, according to multiple eyewitness accounts, he was physically raised from the dead. He appeared to hundreds of people, taught his disciples, and prepared for what was to come.

Forty days after the resurrection, Jesus ascended bodily into the heavens where, according to the Bible, he sits at the right hand of God as the Lord of heaven and earth. Ten days after his ascension, in a gathering of 120 people on the day of Pentecost, a Jewish day of celebration, something truly extraordinary happened. A loud and powerful wind swept over the people gathered. Pillars of what appeared to be fire descended upon the followers of Jesus. The Holy Spirit, the presence and power of God, filled the people, and the church was born. After this, the followers of Jesus went forth and began to do the very things Jesus did—preaching, teaching, and healing—and planting churches and making disciples all over the world. Today, more than two thousand years later, the movement has reached us. This is the Great Awakening, and it has never stopped.

Yes, two thousand years hence and more than two billion followers of Jesus later, this awakening movement of Jesus Christ and his church stands stronger than ever. Billions of ordinary people the world over have discovered in Jesus Christ an awakened life they never imagined possible. They have overcome challenges, defeated addictions, endured untenable hardships and suffering with unexplainable joy, and stared death in the face with the joyful confidence of eternal life. They have healed the sick, gathered the outcasts, embraced the oppressed, loved the poor, contended for justice, labored for peace, cared for the dying, and, yes, even raised the dead.

We all face many challenges and problems. They are deeply personal, yet when joined together, they create enormous and complex chaos in the world, from our hearts to our homes to our churches and our cities. All of this chaos traces to two originating problems: sin and death. Sin, far beyond mere moral failure, describes the fundamental broken condition of every human being. Sin separates us from God and others, distorts and destroys our deepest identity as the image-bearers of God, and poses a fatal problem from which we cannot save ourselves. It results in an ever-diminishing quality of life and ultimately ends in eternal death. Because Jesus lived a life of sinless perfection, he is able to save us from sin and restore us to a right relationship with God, others, and ourselves. He did this through his sacrificial death on the cross on our behalf. Because Jesus rose from the dead, he is able to deliver us from death and bring us into a quality of life both eternal and unending.

This is the gospel of Jesus Christ: pardon from the penalty of sin, freedom from the power of sin, deliverance from the grip of death, and awakening to the supernatural empowerment of the Holy Spirit to live powerfully for the good of others and the glory of God. Jesus asks only that we acknowledge our broken selves as failed sinners, trust him as our Savior, and follow him as our Lord. Following Jesus does not mean an easy life; however, it does lead to a life of power and purpose, joy in the face of suffering, and profound, even world-changing, love for God and people.

All of this is admittedly a lot to take in. Remember, this is an invitation. Will you follow Jesus? Don't let the failings of his followers deter you. Come and see for yourself.

Here's a prayer to get you started:

> Our Father in heaven, it's me (say your name). I want to know you. I want to live an awakened life. I confess I am a sinner. I have failed myself, others, and you in many ways. I know you made me for a purpose, and I want to fulfill that purpose with my one life. I want to follow Jesus Christ. Jesus, thank you for the gift of your life, death, resurrection, and ascension on my behalf. I want to walk in relationship with you as Savior and Lord. Would you lead me into the fullness and newness of life I was made for? I am ready to follow you. Come, Holy Spirit, and fill me with the love, power, and purposes of God. I pray these things by faith in the name of Jesus, amen.

It would be our privilege to help you get started and grow deeper in this awakened life of following Jesus. For some next steps and encouragements visit seedbed.com/awaken.

ABOUT SEEDBED

Seedbed's mission is to gather, connect, and resource the people of God to sow for a great awakening.

Awakening is the outcome of encountering Jesus, by which the love of God the Father is poured into our hearts by the Holy Spirit. Awakening both results from, and leads to:

- renewal of the church,
- evangelization of a generation,
- deep wholeness in people, and
- transformation of society.

The common thread of the Christian story and the great urgency of our day, awakening unfolds in small ways which produce vast blessing to all of creation.

Awakening comes most readily to those who are desperate for more of God, to any disciple of Jesus thirsty for a manner of prayer and quality of relationship that bear the marks of plain, scriptural Christianity—the measure of which is holy love.

The church cannot manufacture awakening; it is ultimately a work of God and a sign of his presence. But we can sow for awakening, remove impediments, and posture ourselves to receive it.

We do so by uniting in travailing prayer, banded discipleship, the ministry of the Word of God and the Holy Spirit, and the bold expansion of God's kingdom.

Learn more at seedbed.com.

Printed by Libri Plureos GmbH in Hamburg, Germany